READY FOR
REFORMATION?

READY FOR REFORMATION?

Bringing Authentic Reform to Southern Baptist Churches

BROADMAN
&HOLMAN
PUBLISHERS

NASHVILLE, TENNESSEE

Ten-Digit ISBN: 0-8054-4059-3
Thirteen-Digit ISBN: 978-0-8054-4059-1

Published by Broadman & Holman Publishers
Nashville, Tennessee

Dewey Decimal Classification: 270
Subject Heading: CHURCH RENEWAL-BAPTISTS
SOUTHERN BAPTISTS

Unless otherwise indicated Scripture text is quoted from the New American Standard Bible, © the Lockman Foundation, 1960, 1962, 1963, 1968, 1971, 1972, 1973, 1975, 1977; used by permission. Other versions are identified as follows: Moffatt, The New Testament, a New Translation by James Moffatt. Copyright © 1964 by James Moffatt. Used by permission of Harper & Row, Inc. and Hodder and Stoughton, Ltd. NEB, The New English Bible, © The Delegates of the Oxford University Press and the Syndics of the Cambridge University Press, 1961, 1970, reprinted by permission. NRSV, New Revised Standard Version of the Bible, copyright © 1989 by the Division of Christian Education of the National Council of Churches of Christ in the United States of America, used by permission, all rights reserved. Phillips, reprinted with permission of Macmillan Publishing Co., Inc. from J. B. Phillips: The New Testament in Modern English, revised edition, © J. B. Phillips 1958, 1960, 1972. RSV, Revised Standard Version of the Bible, copyrighted 1946, 1952, © 1971, 1973.

1 2 3 4 5 6 7 8 9 10   10 09 08 07 06 05

With deep appreciation for their scholarship, genuine piety, love of truth, honest historical methodology, and encouragement to me as a historian, I dedicate this book to the late Drs. Robert A. Baker and W. R. Estep.

Acknowledgments

I thank Len Goss and his helpful and encouraging colleagues at Broadman & Holman. A casual inquiry by him at a Sunday morning worship service led to the completion of this project. The people of Broadman & Holman have indicated a desire to encourage ongoing reformation in Southern Baptist life and were willing to give this book a chance to do that. I hope they will not be disappointed.

Several friends have read the manuscript and given helpful suggestions about form, style, and substance. Among them are Tom Ascol, friend and faithful steward of the gospel for decades; and Peter Beck and Jeff Robinson, astute and aspiring students and future scholars. They have given helpful suggestions in both form and substance. The book sounds a surer and more affirming note because of their observations; its weaknesses may be attributed only to me.

I have learned through more than three and a half decades that I accomplish nothing without the encouragement and helpful involvement of my lovely and beloved wife, Margaret. She gives space, exhortation, personal interest, and enchantment to the day-in, day-out plodding of research and writing. She manages a home with consummate skill in a way that frees the mind from clutter and clatter.

Though all that I have written manifests in many places the personal weaknesses, shortsightedness, prejudices, sinful omissions, and finite limitations of a child of Adam who once was blinded by the god of this age and as yet sees only through a glass darkly, whatever genuine zeal for truth, helpful insight, and edifying brotherly exhortation exists in these pages must be attributed to the persevering grace of God. With a reformation principle that I have not discussed in this book but that must be the conscious intent of all that we do, I invite you to read further.

Soli Deo gloria.

Contents

A Few Names and Words

Adiaphora—Literally, "things indifferent;" the word was used formally by Melancthon, a Lutheran reformer, for certain doctrinal and ceremonial concessions he agreed to make to Roman Catholicism. His proposed concessions caused great controversy. He contended that the areas of concession did not materially affect the purity of worship or the content of the gospel. The controversy in the Church of England between the strict conformist, the Puritan, and the Separatist focused on *adiaphora*. Puritans, Separatists, and eventually Baptists judged *adiaphora* on the basis of the "regulative principle" of biblical authority. We have no authority to introduce as a matter of Christian belief or worship practice what God has forbidden or to go beyond what he has specifically commanded.

American Baptist Churches USA—Known as the Northern Baptist Convention 1907–1950 when they took the name American Baptist Convention. In 1973 they changed the designation to American Baptist Churches USA (ABC-USA).

Antinomianism—Literally, "opposed to the law." It can refer to a great variety of theological teachings that diminish the standing of the Ten Commandments as moral law. These various views affect in different contexts the Bible's teachings on condemnation, justification, holy living (sanctification), and how one may be assured that he or she is a Christian (the doctrine of assurance).

Arian—One who follows a fourth-century heresy that asserted that Jesus was not the eternal Son of God but was the first created being. Through him God created the world, shows the way of redemption, and deems him worthy of worship, but we are not to consider him as having the same nature as the Father. This view was rejected at the Council of Nicea in 325.

Arminianism/Arminius, James (1560–1609)—James Arminius preached and taught in the Reformed Church in Holland. He gradually came to reject some of its distinctive teachings. His followers, known as Arminians, formulated his doctrinal objections with the intent of changing the official teaching of the church. They changed the doctrines of election, calling, atonement, and perseverance. They resisted affirming these as manifestations of God's unilateral sovereignty and unconditioned grace. In their formulation, each reflected a cooperative work between God's grace and the presence of certain humanly generated conditions. Their views were rejected at the Synod of Dort in 1618. The General Baptists of England held an Arminian theology.

Boyce, J. P. (1827–1888)—J. P. Boyce is best known for his work in the founding of the Southern Baptist Theological Seminary. He served as its first chair of the faculty and eventually as its first president. He was president of the Southern Baptist Convention from 1872 to 1879 and again in 1888. He wrote a systematic theology text entitled *Abstract of Systematic Theology*.

Broaddus, Andrew (1770–1848)—Broaddus left his father's Episcopalianism to become a Baptist in 1789. He spent virtually all his ministry in country churches in Virginia, though he was courted strongly by many city churches. He wrote a response to Tom Paine, *The Age of Reason and Revelation* and a response to Alexander Campbell, *The Extra Examined;* opposed the antimission society movement; and greatly encouraged through publication hymn singing in the churches in Virginia.

Broadus, John A. (1827–1895)—Broadus graduated from the University of Virginia in 1850 and served as pastor of the Baptist church in Charlottesville from 1850 until he became a part of the first faculty at the Southern Baptist Theological Seminary. He also wrote *Harmony of the Gospels,* a major contribution to New Testament studies. He also wrote perhaps the single most influential text on preaching—*On the Preparation and Delivery of Sermons.* In 1889, he delivered the Lyman Beecher lectures on preaching at Yale University.

Calvinism—A system of theology reflecting the influence of Augustine, Martin Luther, John Calvin, Ulrich Zwingli, Heinrich Bullinger, and the reformers of the Netherlands. It is called Calvinism because John Calvin (1509–1564) organized its leading principles most clearly and coherently in his systematic theology entitled *The Institutes of the Christian Religion.* Its most distinctive and recognizable ideas were set forth by the Synod of Dort in 1618 under five chapters of doctrine: unconditional election, Christ's atoning work accomplished so as to make certain the salvation of the elect, total depravity, irresistible grace, and perseverance of the saints. Calvinism found its most enduring expression in England and America in the Westminster Confession of Faith (1646).

Carroll, Benajah Harvey (1843–1914)—B. H. Carroll served as pastor of the First Baptist Church of Waco, Texas, 1870–1899. He taught theology and Bible at Baylor from 1872 to 1905. He organized Baylor Theological Seminary in 1905 and moved it to Fort Worth in 1908 when it became Southwestern Baptist Theological Seminary. He served as its president until his death in 1914. His lectures on the English Bible were a staple in his view of theological education. They were published as *An Interpretation of the English Bible.*

Erasmus (1466–1536)—Desiderius Erasmus sought church reform through the application of critical literary principles to the study of the church fathers and the Bible. He advocated a simple and joyous life of piety through following the religious principles of Christ. He approved of Luther's challenge to many of the abuses that existed in Christendom but finally opposed him on his views of justification and the total corruption, and thus bondage, of the human will.

Fosdick, Harry Emerson (1878–1969)—Fosdick caused major controversy in both the Baptist and Presbyterian denominations due to his clearly articulated liberalism. He was an outspoken opponent of fundamentalism and made this known through a widely publicized sermon entitled "Shall the Fundamentalists Win?" in 1922. He gained the ear of the nation through his popular radio program *National Vespers Hour* and through a large number of books. He taught practical theology at Union Theological Seminary in New York from 1908 to 1946 and served as pastor of Riverside Church from 1925 to 1946.

Fuller, Andrew (1754–1815)—Fuller was one of the leaders of the Baptist revival of the late eighteenth and early nineteenth centuries. His *Gospel Worthy of All Acceptation* defended the idea that Calvinism is consistent with absolute human responsibility and, in fact, properly understood, demands the use of every biblically warranted means for the conversion of sinners. His support of William Carey in personal friendship and as secretary of the Baptist Missionary Society was a major contributing factor to the modern missionary movement.

Fuller, Richard (1804–1876)—After a brief practice in law, Richard Fuller became a Baptist preacher. He served for fifteen years as pastor of Beaufort Baptist Church in Beaufort, South Carolina. He moved to Baltimore in 1847 to become pastor of the Seventh Baptist Church. This church founded the Eutaw Place Baptist Church in 1871, and Fuller served as its pastor until his death. He showed marvelous preaching and pastoral skills during the divisive period at Seventh Baptist, when some church members supported the South and its cause and sent their sons to fight for it, while others supported the cause of the Union and sent their sons to fight for it. The church grew from eighty-seven to over twelve hundred during these years.

Furman, Richard (1755–1825)—Furman served as pastor of First Baptist Church of Charleston, South Carolina, from 1787 to 1825. He was a leader in establishing the General Missionary Convention in 1814 and served as its first president. His influence also contributed greatly to the founding of the South Carolina Baptist Convention in 1821. He was a strong preacher, an ardent supporter of the recently established missionary work, and a consistent advocate of ministerial education.

Gambrell, James Bruton (1841–1921)—Known as the "Great Commoner," Gambrell had influence in Baptist life in Mississippi, Georgia, and Texas. He was editor of the *Baptist Record* in Mississippi for sixteen years, president of Mercer University for three years, edited the *Baptist Standard* in Texas for four years, and was active as an officer in the Baptist General Convention of Texas, taught at Southwestern Baptist Theological Seminary, and served as president of the Southern Baptist Convention for four years. Under his leadership the Convention launched the Seventy-Five Million Campaign, precursor to the Cooperative Program.

General Baptists—The first group of modern Baptists originating from English Separatism and influenced by continental Anabaptism. The nomenclature "general" comes from their energetic defense of Arminian theology, including general atonement, election conditioned on foreknown faith, and falling into a lost condition from a true position of salvation.

John Gill (1697–1771)—For over fifty years Gill served the church in London formerly served by Benjamin Keach and eventually served by John Rippon and Charles Spurgeon. A noted self-taught linguist, Gill wrote a commentary on every book of the Bible. He also gave strong and clear defenses of orthodox Christianity against the infidelity and deism of the eighteenth century, defended evangelical theology against "latitunarianism," and defended Calvinism against Arminianism. These battles gave rise to many polemical treatises and a lengthy systematic theology entitled *Body of Divinity*. Many see him as a leading hyper-Calvinist. He held some views, however, out of harmony with hyper-Calvinism.

Hall, Robert, Jr. (1764–1831)—He was one of the most respected, erudite, and truly eloquent preachers of any denomination in the early nineteenth century. He energetically supported the Baptist missionary movement, argued vehemently for freedom of the press, and effectively exposed the weakness of infidelity. His advocacy of open communion in Baptist life led to strong opposition.

Hus, John (1373–1415)—Hus sought reformation of the church in Bohemia and was burned in 1415 for his efforts. Accusations against him included many articles that he was required to recant but that he insisted he never held. Influenced by the writings of Wycliffe, he held to the authority of Scripture. He also opposed the sale of indulgences.

Jeter, Jeremiah Bell (1802–1880)—Jeter spent most of his life in Richmond, Virginia, serving two churches—First Baptist for thirteen years and Grace Street Baptist. He edited the *Religious Herald* for fifteen years and served as the first president of the Foreign Mission Board. He wrote extensive critiques of the theology and influence of Alexander Campbell.

Keach, Benjamin (1640–1704)—Keach changed from being an Arminian [General] Baptist to a Particular [Calvinistic] Baptist persuasion soon after moving to London in 1668. His preaching, expository writing, and theological controversies helped stabilize Baptists during the time of persecution subsequent to the Restoration in 1660. He introduced hymn singing in Baptist worship as a biblically mandated practice. He clearly articulated a biblical defense of consistent church discipline as well as church support for ministers.

Knollys, Hanserd (1598–1691)—Knollys was thrown in prison for leaving a position in the Anglican Church to become a nonconformist. He fled to America after a prison escape, returned to England in 1643, and immediately became active in the early Particular Baptist movement. He preached vigorously in many places, often experienced severe opposition, and on several occasions saw prison doors from the inside. His book of sermons, *Christ Exalted*, is an excellent sampling of the early evangelistic preaching of the Particular Baptists.

Luther, Martin (1483–1546)—More than any other single individual, the Protestant Reformation of the sixteenth century owes its origins to Luther. He challenged not only the financial, moral, and pastoral abuses so notorious for decades if not centuries, but also the doctrinal foundation of papal supremacy, the sacramental system, indulgences, and merit salvation. His biblical and doctrinal expositions restored the principle of *sola scriptura*, clarified the doctrine of justification by faith, secured imputed righteousness as its foundation, and recovered the Augustinian emphasis on human sin and inability and the effectual power of divine grace.

Mallary, C. D. (1801–1864)—Mallary spent his ministerial life serving churches in South Carolina and Georgia. He compiled important biographical works on Edmund Botsford and Jesse Mercer. In 1845, the newly formed Southern Baptist Convention elected him as first corresponding secretary of the Foreign Mission Board, though he was unable to serve for health reasons. He was well-known for his consistent and fervent piety.

Manly, Basil, Jr. (1825–1892)—Manly, a graduate of Princeton Theological Seminary in 1847, served on the first faculty at the Southern Baptist Theological Seminary. He helped establish the first Sunday School Board of the SBC and was the principal author of the *Abstract of Principles*, the confessional statement of the seminary. He also wrote *The Bible Doctrine of Inspiration* at a crucial time for the seminary soon after the Toy controversy.

Molinist—A follower of the teaching of the Spanish Jesuit, Luis Molina (d. 1600). He sought to blend semi-Pelagianism with the teachings of Augustine. He did this by seeking a way to blend God's omniscience, omnipotence, and grace with human free will. God foreknows all that will happen in any given set of circumstances. Out of this exhaustive and absolute precognition, he creates a world in which he knows his will will be accomplished by man's free will in all its complex historical involvements.

Monergism—The salvation of sinners depends from start to finish on the grace of God. Monergism most specifically concerns regeneration—the sinner, being spiritually dead (that is, having nothing intrinsic to his moral nature to produce a positive response to the holy claims of God) and hostile in his mind through wicked works, must be arrested and changed by invincible, omnipotent grace. The sinner, therefore, is considered "passive" at the point of regeneration because while he is dead, he is made alive. Being thus made spiritually alive, he immediately begins a life of positive response to the glory of God as seen particularly in the gospel. The test of a genuine saving work of God is the sinner's desire for, and increasing attainment of, obedience (1 John 3:7–10). On the one hand, we have neither moral power nor attainment of righteousness to initiate or continue any element of salvation. On the other, the continuing operations of God's Spirit sustain within us the desire to reach the holiness for which God has purposed us (2 Cor. 5:5; Phil. 3:12; Rom. 8:8–14).

Particular Baptists—A group of English Baptists that developed around 1638 in London out of English Separatism and Puritanism. They held strong convictions affirming a Calvinist view of salvation. They became the dominant stream of Baptists in England and America.

Pearce, Samuel (1766–1799)—Pearce served as a Particular Baptist pastor in Birmingham, England. He burned with zeal for holiness and souls. Before his untimely death, his energetic support of the missions effort was critical to its sustenance.

Pelagian—Characteristic of Pelagius of the early fifth century. He rejected the doctrine of original sin and consequently believed that humanity maintained an ability to keep the law and even respond without sin to natural revelation. His views were opposed with increasing clarity and fervor by Augustine throughout his life.

Pepper, George D. (1833–1913)—A graduate of Newton Theological Seminary, he served as a pastor in Maine before assuming the chair of ecclesiastical history at Newton in 1865. In 1868 he accepted the professorship of Christian Theology at Crozer Theological Seminary.

Philadelphia Association—The first Baptist Association in America, established in 1707. This highly influential association adopted the 1689 Baptist Confession as its doctrinal standard and expected all its member churches to approve it enthusiastically. It lent preaching aid to destitute churches, sent evangelists into unchurched settlements, and supported the missionary movement.

Ryland, John, Jr. (1753–1825)—Ryland was a part of the group with Carey, Fuller, Pearce, and John Sutcliff that launched the missionary movement among the Particular Baptists, and he succeeded Andrew Fuller as its secretary. It fell his responsibility to collect and edit the memoir entitled *The Life and Death of the Reverend Andrew Fuller.* He wrote with strong conviction for evangelical Calvinism and against antinomianism and hyper-Calvinism. When president of Bristol Academy, he upgraded its academic status to college level.

Sandemanian—Characteristic of the views of Robert Sandeman (1718–1771). Preeminently this refers to his view of faith that he defined as mere assent to the proposition that Jesus Christ is the Son of God. He believed that the Calvinist view that faith must follow regeneration in order to have the true aspect of trust made faith a good work and thus contradicted the doctrine of justification by faith alone.

Schleiermacher, Friederich D. E. (1768–1834)—A German theologian who wrote a systematic theology for the Romantic movement. For him theology was not the coherent expression of objective revealed truth from God but the expression of man's sense of the infinite. Religion flows from our deepest consciousness of absolute dependence. Jesus leads us to God because he more than any other person lived from a pure and profound sense of his dependence.

Semi-Pelagian—A system of theology that developed in the Middle Ages. It asserted that though man needed grace, he maintained a spark of ability to take a step toward God to which God would respond with grace, and increasingly so with each new movement toward God made by the sincere seeker.

Smyth, John (d. 1612)—Smyth led a group of Separatists from England to Holland in 1608. While there he led his congregation to adopt believer's baptism. He gave a detailed discussion of the reasons for this in a book entitled *Character of the Beast*. They also changed their theology from Calvinism to Arminianism. When Smyth decided that the church should unite with the Mennonites, a small remnant broke with the church and returned to England. Led by Thomas Helwys, this small congregation became the first Baptist church in England.

Socinian—One who follows the heresy of Faustus Socinus (1539–1604), who taught that Jesus was only a man. According to Socinus, Jesus had a deeper sense of the common divine sonship we all share and is thus the path to fellowship with the Father. His teaching anticipated modern Unitarianism.

Spilsbury, John (1593–1668)—Spilsbury [or Spilsbery] served as pastor of the first Particular Baptist church. He strongly opposed infant baptism and Arminianism. He did not think a church could exist without a clearly stated public confession of faith. His influence is largely responsible for the production of the confession of faith produced by the Particular Baptist churches of London in 1644.

Spurgeon, Charles (1834–1892)—Spurgeon served as pastor of the Metropolitan Tabernacle in London from 1854 to 1892. After a two-year ministry in a rural congregation at Waterbeach, Spurgeon moved to London in February 1854. His steady stream of published sermons, week after week and year after year in book form (*The New Park Street Pulpit* and the *Metropolitan Tabernacle Pulpit*) is an astounding and formidable accomplishment. He also published a monthly paper of sermons, articles, reviews, news, and spiritual encouragement entitled *The Sword and Trowel*. His massive accomplishments in evangelism are puzzling to many who think that his aggressive and clearly articulated Calvinism would minimize such zeal and success. In 1889 he separated from the Baptist Union over its refusal to deal with the growth of liberalism in its ranks.

Synergism—This comes from two Greek words that mean "to work with." Doctrinally it means that the human will initiates the new birth. God provides the occasion by the convicting agency of the Holy Spirit, but regeneration does not take place until a sinner repents of sin and believes in Christ. This construct continues throughout the stages of salvation so that in some sense human consent is necessary to effect the completion of what God has begun or made available in salvation. All Christians believe that salvation involves good works. In synergism, these good works are seen not only as a response to God's operations of grace but also in some sense meritorious of greater grace.

Taylor, Dan (1738–1813)—Taylor was converted under the preaching of the Wesleyans. His disagreement with them on baptism led him to join the General Baptists. When he learned that they tolerated Socinianism and failed to preach a truly substitutionary atonement, he led in the formation of a New Connection of General Baptists in 1770. He published a large number of works on foundational Christian issues and engaged in controversy with Andrew Fuller when Fuller contended that Calvinism was consistent with a universal gospel appeal to sinners.

Warrant to believe—This phrase occurs frequently in Puritan literature and in the hyper-Calvinist controversy. On what basis may a sinner assume freedom to come to Christ for salvation? The hyper-Calvinist says this warrant comes from an internal confidence that he is being effectually called and is therefore one of God's elect. The Arminian says a warrant to believe is only in a doctrine of the universality of Christ's atoning death, the universality of the redemptive love of God, and universal operations of the Holy Spirit in calling. The evangelical Calvinist says the warrant comes from the open and general invitation of the gospel message itself.

Wayland, Francis (1796–1865)—Massively influential Baptist in New England. He was president of Brown University from 1827 to 1855. Early in his ministry he served as pastor of First Baptist Church in Boston. After he resigned as president at Brown, he served the First Baptist Church of Providence. He was a strong supporter of the foreign mission work, a great admirer of Adoniram Judson, and one of the foremost educators in America.

Wycliffe, John (1329–1384)—Wycliffe has been called the "Morning Star of the Reformation." A graduate of Oxford, he also lectured there for many years. He became alienated from the papacy and believed that monastic orders should be abolished. He argued that Scripture alone should be the final authority for thought, conduct, and church life, and he organized a group to translate the Latin Vulgate into English. He denied transubstantiation. He strongly emphasized an Augustinian view of grace. His writings influenced Luther by way of John Hus. The Council of Constance (1414–1418) ordered his body to be exhumed, burned, and thrown into a river. This was done in 1428.

Introduction

Jerry Sutton has called the conservative resurgence in the Southern Baptist Convention a Reformation.[1] This is a helpful designation—ambitious, but helpful. Sutton argues the need for reformation through a brief analysis of the theological and institutional status of Southern Baptist life in the two decades prior to 1979. He chronicles the development of the theological challenge in the inerrancy controversy year by year. He then documents the changes pursued in institutional life in the SBC. His evaluation of the condition of the Convention immediately following the conservative victory employed the nomenclature "marks of vitality." His discussion of "Distractions" pointed mainly to continuing skirmishes arising from disenfranchised moderates. His "Challenge for the Future" focused on a vision of "enormous growth," while his parting line was, "From the standpoint of conservatives, truth has triumphed."[2]

His book embodies a refreshingly positive and theologically conservative perspective. Those who agree with what happened can be heartened by the overview of what must be seen as a merciful providence of God in reclaiming a stewardship almost forsaken. Many books have been written from a radically different perspective. The resurgence has been interpreted through many grids from a socio-cultural reaction to an aggressive and hostile assault on healthy and effective Baptist institutions.[3] Sutton, by contrast, interprets the movement as a needed corrective motivated by biblically derived theological conviction.

Denominational life has many analogies to individual Christian life. As a Christian should find encouragement in evidence of real sanctification, so a denomination may enjoy evidence of serious faithfulness to a corporate spiritual task. An individual, however, who ignores the power of indwelling sin becomes susceptible to

1

a fall or at least to blindness to areas of life that need mortification and revival. A denomination that rests too quickly from self-examination or becomes self-congratulatory will often ignore areas of weakness and will sometimes even exult in practices that actually are destructive in their tendency.

In this book I assume that a genuine movement of God's Spirit has initiated a reformation among Southern Baptists. Reformation involves much more, however, than the mere recovery of biblical authority. Reformation penetrates the deep recesses of theological self-perception and purpose in institutions. It involves time, patience, sacrifice, and honest self-criticism. For Baptists this does not require as much new work as the sixteenth-century Reformation did; it does, however, involve a serious reengagement with doctrinal and practical ideas of the past. Refusal to use the clean sea breeze of the past to help purify the present may result in an aborted reformation.

May the Lord continue to revive his work, and may he bring it to completion until the day of Christ Jesus.

Chapter 1

Remember from Where You Have Fallen

Jehu—a Reformation Failure

"Come with me, and see my zeal for the LORD," said Jehu to Jehonadab (2 Kings 10:16). And indeed, like Elijah the prophet just a few years before, he had been very zealous for the Lord God of Hosts. Already he had slain, in direct obedience to his commission (2 Kings 9:7–10) the king of the Northern Kingdom, Joram, as well as the Ahab-influenced king of the Southern Kingdom, Ahaziah. Jezebel had met her prophesied death in all its inglorious and dark dimensions. The heads of the seventy sons of Ahab had been presented to Jehu in baskets. From the south, forty-two relatives of Ahab and Jezebel had fallen into the hands of Jehu, who slaughtered them. Now, at the time he invited Jehonadab to join him, he sped to Samaria to kill all who belonged to Ahab there, as he had done in Jezreel. In addition, he used cunning to gather together all the worshippers of Baal into one place and arranged for their slaughter: "Thus Jehu destroyed Baal out of Israel" (2 Kings 10:28 KJV).

So much done! His anointed commission completed. The grotesque and brutal reign of the house of Ahab ended and the prophets killed by Jezebel avenged. Naboth, murdered for his vineyard, crying from the ground, saw the blood of the

3

house of Ahab spilled in exquisite justice. "Because thou hast done well in executing that which is right in mine eyes, and hast done unto the house of Ahab according to all that was in mine heart," so spoke Jehovah to Jehu (2 Kings 10:30 KJV). Enough? No. With such punctilious fulfillment of his commission in ridding the kingdom of its lingering and gross injustices and the perverted worship of Baal, Jehu fell short of the necessary reform: "He departed not from the sins of Jeroboam, which made Israel to sin" (2 Kings 10:31 KJV).

Jeroboam, according to 1 Kings 12, led Israel to sin by establishing alternate places of worship and ordaining an unqualified priesthood. He sought to represent Jehovah with graven images of his own devising. He established as cultic practice forms "which he had devised in his own heart" (1 Kings 12:33). Had Jehu completed the reformation needed, he would have instructed all Israel to go to Jerusalem to the appointed feasts and participate in the appointed sacrifices, even if it meant loss of the kingdom from his control. He had lopped off the branches of the sins of Israel, but the root he left undisturbed.

Essential Aspects of Reformation

Such danger stares into the face of any reformation. Most attempts at reform of the church in the late Middle Ages dealt only with symptoms. Clerical ignorance and immorality, priestly cupidity, ministerial absenteeism from parishes, the intensified grasp of the papacy for worldly power, financial abuses of the most egregious and cunning sort, an ignorant and neglected laity, the proliferation of mendicants in the church orders, a schism in the papacy itself, and controversy over the proper location of the papacy—all these threatened the dignity of the church and needed to be addressed. If all had been solved, however, the real need of reformation would still have been untouched.

Two issues—the authority of Scripture alone and the sovereignty of God in salvation—formed the foundation of spiritual life that lay untapped beneath the surface of much late medieval dissent. Luther, perhaps taking his cue from Wycliffe and Hus, saw this clearly. He addressed the problem at that depth. When Erasmus finally decided to take up the pen against Luther, Luther found great satisfaction in the arena in which he was challenged. He congratulated Erasmus on his grasp of the real issue of Luther's challenge to the church of Rome. He refused to dabble over mere temporal perversities or the bellies of the monks, though these were not entirely inconsequential. He went to the heart of the controversy—the nature of the human will in its relation to sin and grace.

This debate with Erasmus over the bondage of the will forced two issues to the surface over and over: (1) rigorous exegesis of Scripture dictates our understanding of doctrine, and (2) as sinful creatures enslaved to sin, we proclaim a gospel established on God's sovereign mercies and Christ's completed merits. So fundamental were these ideas to the Reformation that one emerged as the "formal principle"—that is, all doctrines and practices must be developed, or formed, from direct biblical authority.

The other became known as the "material principle"—the actual doctrines built upon the formal principle. In this case the doctrinal construction that constituted the substantial difference between Roman Catholicism and Protestantism was justification by faith. As the Reformers developed the doctrine of justification, it necessarily assumed the bondage of the human will and, consequently, the sovereign and effectual mercies of God in Christ.

The Reformers knew that reformation—deeply theological, intensely personal, and pervasively institutional—was necessary. They also had confidence that they had devoted themselves to the right issues. They never exhibited confidence that they had completed all that needed to be done. They lived under the motivation of the truth that the reformed church must always be reforming—*ecclesia reformata semper reformanda.*

Southern Baptists on the Brink

Now we must ask, "Have Southern Baptists reached the root issue of reformation in their quest for a renewed church life?" Like Jehu, with an uncompromising determination they have amputated the more grotesque appendages of corruption. The first blow fell with shattering accuracy on the issue of inerrancy. This fell with such effectiveness that a clearly observable change occurred in denominational life. Before 1979, one rarely could find a denominational servant who gave uncompromised adherence to inerrancy as a personal conviction and asserted its necessity for a clear and certain formulation of Christian faith. Since that time this conviction is virtually universal in Southern Baptist institutional life. The formal principle, at least from the standpoint of the assertion of authority, has been well articulated. Whether this principle will be allowed to operate powerfully in matters of worship and discipline remains to be seen.

Baptists developed their practice of biblical authority in light of the regulative principle—that is, God has regulated what is to be believed and how we should worship him, and we have no warrant or prerogative to go beyond what he has revealed. Some implications of this idea form one of the main concerns of this book.

The material principle, however, has a more checkered history of recovery. This means that a foundational issue with large results still lingers in the wings of the reformation stage, waiting for a cue to appear before its historically obligated panel of reviewers. The libretto has been well formulated for years, dusty from indifference, waiting for a troupe to learn its lines couched in such august chapter heads as "Of Christ the Mediator," or "Of Free Will," or "Of Effectual Calling," or "Of Repentance unto Life and Salvation," or "Of Grace in Regeneration," or "Of God's Purpose of Grace." Will such a call come, or will Baptists seek to produce "Pilgrim's Progress" while eliminating the parts of "Evangelist" and "Faithful"? This book will, in part, seek to explore the material principle in its historical manifestations in Baptist life along with some of the practical outworkings of that biblical issue.

An Early Reformation Proposal

The danger, of course, is that which infiltrates all good and earnest beginnings at reformation, religious or political. When the disenfranchised reformers finally gain ascendancy, the feeling of power and privilege cuts short many of the former ideals. While indebted to the churches and responsible as stewards of the mysteries of God, a culture of preeminence and control can be created into which few may penetrate. One of the main observations brought to bear on Southern Baptist Convention personnel prior to the effected changes was the inability to be self-critical or to allow the media within Convention life to have freedom as objective analysts and reporters of news.

These tensions formed the content of one of the Shophar Papers of 1980 written by Paige Patterson. Patterson noted that "denominational executive offices can become 'Protestant Meccas' to which all must bow, with 'programs' being substituted for righteousness." Any questions or doubts make a person susceptible to anathemas by "those who claim to be 'loyal.'"[1] He pointed to three problematic areas.

First, "Only the literature published by the official publishing agency of the denomination may be used." Churches that for very good reasons might choose to use other literature "face the probability of pressure and even harassment. Where are our Baptist liberties?"

Second, though Patterson defended the Cooperative Program as a legitimate and useful denominational response to the clear biblical precedent of "association" in Acts 15 and other aspects of biblical warrant, he clearly believed that it had been elevated to a position of holiness. Diverting funds into any other ways of doing missions constituted, according to the so-called Baptist Meccas, a challenge to the Great Commission and Baptist principles. Churches creating optional mission emphases were labeled as disloyal and their ministers as unworthy of denominational recognition.

Third, "Denominational periodicals," Patterson warned, "can become responsible primarily for 'defending the denomination' rather than for accurate, unbiased, thoroughly researched presentation of news and truth." When the press reduces itself to mere denominational promotion, it loses the ability to be a sanctifying influence on Convention programs and structures. The press also becomes adversarial to anyone, whether church or individual, that questions Convention policy and practice.

Patterson wanted a new kind of denominationalism. He called for openness that is servant to and not master of the churches, meaningful deliberation among a wider spectrum of concerned people, and a more open system of Convention operations in selection of personnel to avoid the old system of king makers. These seem to be desirable patterns to pursue. "When priorities are set without regard to biblical revelation, the seeds of decadence are planted. If loyalty becomes equated with silent consent to programs, however noble, the stench of encroaching death will be evident."[2]

Challenges to Reformation Progress

Patterson shared the experience of many theological students of the 1960s and 1970s. They grew weary of the spiritual devastation they experienced and lamented their instructors' preference for personal freedom above the biblical text. A simple recovery, therefore, of the conviction that the text holds sole and absolute authority seems to be an indescribable blessing. And it is!

The difference between believing or not believing in a divinely inspired Bible is substantial. The former position determines that the text rules because God has spoken; the latter subjects the text to the reader's experience because the text itself is purely the product of—thus never rising above—human experience. On that basis the redefinition of Christianity in general and Baptist life in particular had proceeded. Moving forward unchallenged and unabated, the process came dangerously close to a thorough makeover of both. In some cases the metamorphosis was complete.

But at just the right time, the challenge occurred. Paul informed Timothy that God would protect his deposit of truth until "that day." The most likely translation of 2 Timothy 1:12, contextually considered, is, "I am convinced that he is able to guard my deposit, that is, the deposit he entrusted to me, until that day." He then admonished Timothy, in that confidence, to retain the standard of sound words and guard through the Holy Spirit the treasure entrusted to him. God will not allow his deposited treasure to disappear either in authority or content. It is possible that we live in a time of the merciful providence of God in which that deposit has been reclaimed.

The warnings that Patterson issued in the initial glow of challenge to the dominant theological and administrative culture of the Convention do not lose their relevance when the doctrinal stance of denominational leadership changes toward conservatism. Some would wonder if the "king-maker" operations that he detested and criticized are once again firmly entrenched. While doctrinal recovery provides firmer ground for powerful and effective voluntary union, a system of checks and balances that defies the tendency for a top-heavy denomination should be carefully observed. Apart from this, the tendency of power to corrupt may again prove to be too overwhelming.

Seats of control may be just as alluring to the confessionally orthodox as to the doctrinal latitudinarian. And, ironically, the gaining of control, particularly when combined with a restricted theological vision, might serve to arrest further doctrinal reform.

Overall, while recovery has been substantial, the work is not yet done. Inerrancy now rules the consciences of a vast majority of local church pastors, and in a much better informed way, and inerrantists seem well-entrenched in leadership positions at seminaries, mission boards, and other strategic agencies and organizations. Inerrantists are everywhere. Perhaps even some who were not inerrantists now genuflect to the term, if not the idea, and desire a nonconfrontational peaceful coexistence with the present leadership. Some pockets of strength for *The Way We Were*[3] work feverishly to impede if not destroy the growing hegemony of the inerrancy party, but for the most part they must settle for much less than they want.

A greater danger, however, than the settling of leadership and the guerrilla warfare of the deposed looms menacingly near. Perhaps always parallel with the need for ever-expanding discussion of pertinent doctrinal matters is the ongoing conflict with the world, the flesh, and the devil. This war for the soul challenges every Christian with the daily need for abundance of real knowledge and discernment, self-examination, and purposeful mortification. External reformation may be destroyed or rendered meaningless unless, contrary to the settled satisfaction of Jehu, it provokes us to "cleanse ourselves from all defilement of flesh and spirit, perfecting holiness in the fear of God" (2 Cor. 7:1).

A profession that has a form of godliness but denies its power to make alive and make holy just as clearly detracts from the glory of God as does heresy. The gravitational pull of our flesh into the mire of unrighteousness constantly seeks to seize us either personally or systemically. The call of gospel grace, as well as its intrinsic impulse, still speaks thus: "Now having been freed from sin and enslaved to God, you derive your benefit, resulting in sanctification, and the outcome, eternal life" (Rom. 6:22). External reform never substitutes for holiness. It should, however, constitute the substantive and conceptual power for the purification of the churches. The final chapter of this book explores the relation of doctrine and devotion in producing God-centered persons.

Premature satisfaction presents another danger to reformation. As true godliness both individually and corporately only increases by expansive understanding, external reform must proceed, driven by an increasingly encyclopedic doctrinal clarity. The gains made must be conserved, and new issues must be addressed. Truth still cries aloud in the street for those who will buy her and sell her not. Initial success in foundational repair does not suffice for the whole but makes further progress possible. In fact, the partial nature of a completed foundation begs for a fitting superstructure. A candid recognition that other issues call for attention only highlights the remarkable shift of direction. Recovery of the authority of the Word calls for celebration but just as surely requires careful but unrelenting extension (Ezra 3:10–13).

The task of reclaiming, therefore, is not complete. If only the acceptance of the divine *authority* of the deposit gains adherence but the *content* of the treasure itself

9

lies dormant, the recovery is a sham. The formal principle without the material principle does not make a reformation. For recovery or reformation to be full, the content of the revelation must also be rediscovered and proclaimed. As one section of this book will argue, renewed attention to a sweeping historic confessional theology will inspire broader and deeper apprehension of truth and more love for God and the brethren.

A Challenging Biblical Image

The accounts in Ezra and Nehemiah of the return from Babylonian exile provide a biblical model for reformation, its complexity, and the great variety of responses to it. Upon the rediscovery of the law under Ezra and Nehemiah, the people of Israel immediately celebrated the Feast of Booths, which had been ignored since the time of Joshua. In addition, they vowed to make provision for faithful adherence to all religious festivals and sacrifices (Ezra 8:13–18; 10:28–39). In Ezra 3, when the foundation of the temple had been restored, the rejoicing could hardly be discerned from the crying by those who had seen the first temple. How tragically the glory had departed was revealed to them as they realized how far a foundation was from a completed temple. Even so, after a systematic razing of a historic doctrinal edifice, the restoration of the foundation evoked praise and weeping. The beauty of what was stood no more, but a foundation for its restoration now stood firmly in place.

The full shining of truth after its eclipse brings to light many breaches in the wall in need of repair. Neither Baptist evangelism nor ecclesiology can stand in isolation from the rest of Christian truth. For a truly "Baptist" ecclesiology to be coherent, it must arise from the whole counsel of God. In defending it, Baptists must be able to give an account about how their views of the church fully reflect the whole system of biblical truth. A reformation of Baptist identity will involve a serious reengagement at least of the ideas discussed in the following chapters.

Even when fully restored, however, conscious attention to these ideas must necessarily continue. They are not truths to be pursued only in times of decline and emergency but ongoing elements of Christian profession, not only *worthy* of closest attention but *necessary* for Christian faith and practice.

Malachi gives witness to how quickly the gains of reformation and restoration can be lost. "The priest's lips should keep knowledge, and they should seek the law at his mouth," the Lord told Judah. "But ye are departed out of the way"

(Mal. 2:7–8 KJV). Even after the recent time of restoration and reformation, they had begun to pervert worship by ignoring the specific requirement of God (chap. 1); the priesthood lost its purity and faithfulness in giving exposition of the written word of divine revelation (2:1–11); they had shown disregard for the covenantal privileges of the nation by violations of marriage vows (2:11–16); they had questioned the character of God and spread doubt about his justice by carping against his providence (2:17; 3:13–15); they had ignored the special status of a God-ordained ministry among them by ignoring the necessary provisions for them (3:8–10). How quickly reformation can fizzle if not pursued with a self-critical and God-focused zeal!

The following pages suggest several areas for expanding, energetic, and brotherly conversation. We are not so naïve as to pine for the good old days. But one must recognize that the doctrinal clarity and practical concerns of a previous generation were shoved aside into a foggy marshland by the expansive but decreasingly doctrinal denominationalism of the middle sixties years of the twentieth century. A reintroduction of many of these ideas and the healthy discussions attached to them might frighten some as a harbinger of division. In reality, sober involvement with these issues holds promise for greater purity of fellowship and purpose and promotes a stronger, more singular witness in the world.

Chapter 2

The Health of Confessional Christianity

A quest for individual freedom gradually eroded organized doctrine for about six decades of the twentieth century. It can be argued that the adoption of the *Baptist Faith and Message* in 1925 by the Southern Baptist Convention greatly impeded the progress of a liberalization that had swamped the Northern Baptist Convention in the previous two decades. Nevertheless, several factors conspired to move Southern Baptists in the same direction but at a greatly decreased pace. Denominationalism isolation with increased denominational efficiency produced an overconfidence in safety and an increasing carelessness about issues of doctrine. Pragmatism and fervor for unity cleared the way for doctrinal insipidity and increasing aggressiveness of heterodoxy. Baptists, as a testimony to their belief in the clarity and infallibility of Scripture, must recapture with candor and honesty the love for consistent, coherent truth that characterized the days of beginning and development. The material principle of reformation depends so thoroughly on the congruence of the whole fabric of theology that it can find life only in the presence of a revival of detailed, biblically full, carefully and faithfully organized confessional theology.

The Protestant Reformation, including the rise of Baptists, produced an abundance of confessions. They served several purposes. First, they underlined points of agreement with historic orthodox Christianity. Second, they clearly defined the doctrines of the gospel in opposition to the prevailing Roman Catholicism. Third, they clarified differences, mainly on the church and ordinances, and provided talking points between the developing Reformation churches. Fourth, they served as helpful teaching aids for maintaining purity and unity within and among the churches. For three centuries Baptists used confessions in the same way. The growing influence of the *Baptist Faith and Message* since it was newly revised in 2000 indicates positive change consistent with Baptist historical development.

Present from the Beginning

John Spilsbury (1593–1668), pastor of the first Particular Baptist church that arose in seventeenth-century England, reasoned from Scripture that formation of a local church required a confession of faith. Apart from a confession of faith, no covenantal commitment could exist as the foundation for constituting a visible congregation. Only in this way can a group know if they share a common experience and have been shaped by the truth of God's Word toward the same end. Covenanting individuals should know if their goals in worship, witness, and teaching are the same. Adherence to a confession demonstrates a necessary unity.

Even when he had reduced his doctrinal expectations to a minimum, John Smyth still gave witness to a confession of faith as the basis for his willingness to unite with others and consider them his brothers in Christ. Although he maintained to the end that true Christians and the openly wicked should not mingle in one congregation, he would no longer call true believers anti-Christian, though they might be in impure churches. He stated:

> The articles of Religion which are the ground of my salvation, at these, wherin I differ from no Good Christian: That Jesus Christ, the Sonne of God, and the Sonne of Marie, is the Anointed King, Priest, and Prophett of the church, the onlie mediator of the new Testament, and that through true repentance and faith in him who alone is our saviour, wee receive remission of sinnes, and the holie ghost in this lyfe, and there-with all the redemption of our bodies, and everlastinge lyfe in the resurrection of the bodie: and whosoever walketh according to this rule, I must needs acknowledge him my brother: yea, although he differ from me in divers other particulars.[1]

Though minimal in its content, Smyth still expected a clear expression of a distinctive view of Christ, repentance from sin and faith in him, the presence of the Holy Spirit, and the resurrection of the body.

A Servant of the Bible

Confessions do not replace the Bible; they express biblical truth. Andrew Fuller (1754–1815), no novice in the arena of theological dispute, expressed the obvious choices on this issue: "If the articles of faith be opposed to the authority of Scripture, or substituted in the place of such authority, they become objectionable and injurious; but if they simply express the united judgment of those who voluntarily subscribe them, they are incapable of any such kind of imputation."[2]

These expositions have been used to declare faith, to test its existence in others, and to encourage study of the Bible. Confessions serve to organize and extend biblical exposition. When one interprets a passage of Scripture, he distills from that passage certain propositions that he considers true, since they are accurate expressions of the biblical text. Next, these separate expository truths find fuller expression in their synthetic organization into a biblical "doctrine." All that the Bible has to say about God's dealing with sinners in a gracious way may be organized into the biblical doctrine of salvation. Texts from Genesis to Revelation define and nuance the doctrine; the organized presentation of it would not detract from biblical truth but would give powerful expression to it.

Not only exposition and synthesis but internal connection as well should characterize a useful confession. Synthesis connects Scriptures on the same subject with one another to form a doctrine. These doctrines then must be described in such a way to demonstrate that unbroken streams of truth flow into a mighty river of truth. Each developed doctrine plays its part in giving expression to the one faith expressed in the whole of divine revelation. The doctrine of sin may not be separated from the doctrine of redemption which in turn flows from the doctrine of the work of Christ which cannot be understood in its fullness apart from Christ's person.

All of these point to the wisdom and purpose of God and the flow of all history to that great confession of all creation, "Jesus Christ is Lord" (Phil. 2:11 KJV). This shout will shatter history and express the glory of God. Its truth will be expressed in even more compelling dimensions as he speaks to some, "I never knew you; depart from me, you evildoers" (Matt. 7:23 RSV; cf. 25:41), and to others,

"Come, you who are blessed of My Father, inherit the kingdom prepared for you from the foundation of the world" (Matt. 25:34).

In the absence of such a system of thought, a Christian, as Andrew Fuller expresses it, will have "only a few loose, unconnected thoughts, without entering into the harmony and glory of the gospel."[3] Instead of such a disorderly approach, would it not be more honoring to God and more faithfully reflect his nature as a revealing and redeeming God to have a clear statement of faith? Would not a confession more accurately express confidence that the revelation of redemptive truth and purpose has reached its fruition in Christ? This revelation that came only gradually and through a variety of mediums in times past has now culminated and reached maturity and finality in the person and work of Christ.

How fitting to give as full expression as possible to what we believe is the final shape of the redemptive revelation of God! "Every well-informed and consistent believer, therefore," Fuller agrees, "must have a creed—a system which he supposes to contain the leading principles of Divine revelation."[4]

They Are Amendable

These are man-made documents. Consequently, no final authority may be claimed for them. They may be changed as new understandings arise or new challenges call for the organized expression of a biblical truth. The doctrine of creation has called for the addition of new affirmations in light of the challenge of scientific materialism. Technology and the sexual revolution call for confessional statements about the biblical view of sexuality, the origin and value of life, and the nature of the family. Providential events often cause the church to give new energy to understanding the Bible's view of a topic not envisioned by previous generations. At times creeds have contained affirmations that needed alteration in light of greater clarity of truth or insufficient or misleading expressions contained in the creed. Again Fuller comments on this phenomenon.

> The fallibility of all human judgment is fully allowed. A Christian society, as well as an individual, is liable to err in judging what are the doctrines and precepts of Christ. Whatever articles of faith and practice, therefore, are introduced into a community, they ought, no doubt, to be open to correction or amendment, whenever those who subscribe them shall perceive their inconsistency with the will of Christ.[5]

15

During the early days of the seventeenth century, ecclesiological discussions abounded, and differing views of church order emerged rapidly within English Protestantism. John Smyth made several changes in his ecclesiology and with each change altered his confessional statement. When charged with inconsistency for so many and such rapid shifts, he responded, "I professe I have changed, and shall be readie still to change, for the better: and if it be ther glorie to be peremptorie and immutable, in ther articles of Religion, they may injoye that glorie without my envie, though not without the grief of my hart for them."[6]

As Smyth moved from a state church formed by infant baptism to a free church and believers' church formed by believer's baptism, he felt he should publish the truth as he understood it and mark his convictions by a confession. Smith considered an unwillingness to change toward the truth and to confess such a change as perverse in a Christian.

Abraham Booth (1734–1806) knew well the possibility of changing the leading themes of one's confessional commitment. In addition to his rejection of infant baptism, Smyth had rejected Calvinism; Booth moved the other direction. Initially Booth ministered within General Baptist life. He wrote a sarcastic polemical poem against Calvinism entitled *Absolute Predestination*. According to his own testimony, this effort at opposing "the doctrine of sovereign and distinguishing grace" reflected the "ignorance of his mind, the pride of his heart, and the prejudice of his education." His mind soon changed as through impartial inquiry and prayer he found sovereign grace to be "a doctrine of the Bible, and a dictate of the unerring Spirit." He deeply regretted his ill-conceived performance.

"As a poem, if considered in a critical light," Booth judged, "it is despicable; if in a theological view, detestable." But he was not through yet. "As it is an impotent attack on the honour of divine grace, in respect to its glorious freeness, and a bold opposition to the sovereignty of God, and as such I renounce it."[7] As a man of inflexible honesty and uncompromising principle, he informed his congregation of his change and separated from his people.

Booth's work with a small group for five or six years led to his composing the book *Reign of Grace* in 1768. A young Southern Baptist scholar, B. A. Copass, discovered this book in 1900. He wrote E. Y. Mullins to give him an evaluation of it and encouraged him to make his students acquainted with it.

> I venture to call your attention to a book that has greatly blessed me. In my opinion it is one of the strongest books in existence. I refer

to "The Reign of Grace" by Abraham Booth. He has the flavor of Owen etc., those old men who believe something in regard to grace. And yet he has clearness of statement and arrangement. . . . It seems to me that it would help any student of the systematic theology class to carefully study [sic] it. His definitions are concise and clear, I think much superior to those in your text-book in theology. I would want it by my side when I came to "election," "calling," justification etc. Possibly you are acquainted with it and if so I write uselessly. In any case it has helped me, and I believe will help settle the opinions of any young student in this time when so little is made of God's sovereign grace.[8]

The publication of Booth's *Reign of Grace* drew the attention of the Prescott Street church in London to him. The next year at their request Booth became their pastor. At his installation and ordination to the ministry there, he presented a confession of faith, outlining clearly the distinguishing Baptist and Calvinistic doctrines. After presenting this confession, he closed with the testimony that he had "experienced their powerful, comforting, sanctifying influence on my own soul." Nevertheless, he did not "pretend to infallibility of judgment" or to know "all that may be known in the present imperfect state, concerning God or his will" or Christ and his kingdom. He professed his desire, therefore, "to have a mind open to conviction, and susceptive of truth." When God led him to such further discoveries, he promised "to communicate it to others as cases and circumstances may require."[9] He had done it before.

Certain themes of the Bible, however, emerge as inextricably central to its message and undeniably clear in their basic content. Their expressions in confessional terms do not await a lengthy providential provocation. The doctrines of God, creation, mankind, sin, redemption, the person and work of Christ, judgment, heaven and hell bear so heavily on the central purpose of Scripture that they have appeared as items of confession from the beginning. Their clarity has been increasing through the centuries as controversy has brought about purification of vocabulary and concept. Their confessional history has produced such profound enunciation of the doctrine that little change may be expected or even tolerated. Reaffirmation of these clearly defined doctrines must be a part of true reformation. Several of these heads of doctrine have indeed been reaffirmed in clearer, more uncompromising terms in the *Baptist Faith and Message* adopted in 2000 by the Southern Baptist Convention.

History Endorses Confessions

Some historians believe that the genius of Baptist life is in its freedom from doctrinal parameters. "Baptists are a freedom-based group of Christians for whom voluntarism, nonconformity, and dissent, are essential elements of faith." They prefer to call confessional unity a "mindless robotic conformity to someone else's notions about faith."[10] Another, pronouncing purposefully a caricature of grotesque proportions, paints a picture of confessions that many think is accurate: "rigid, one-sided, inquisitorial dogmatism."[11]

These strong characterizations do not reflect accurately the historical picture. This increased sense of confessional responsibility evidenced in the *Baptist Faith and Message* is consistent with the larger picture of historical Baptist identity. Baptist history has not been short on such confessions or on high confidence in their usefulness. Individuals, churches, associations, and larger denominational structures have produced confessions. John Smyth, John Spilsbury, Thomas Collier, John Gill, Abraham Booth, Andrew Fuller, John Clarke, Obadiah Holmes, Isaac Backus, John Leland, Spencer Cone, and others have produced personal confessions of faith which they were glad to publish to the world to show their agreement with other Christians and to define a specific stance which they felt they could relinquish only under the guilt of the blood of souls.

Churches established confessions by which they defined their mission and disciplined their membership. William Stokes wrote an essay on creeds that the Midland Association published in its two-hundredth anniversary history. Stokes, from Birmingham, argued that "it is not enough, therefore, that a man declares that he believes the Bible." Christian communities have not only a right but an obligation to ask in what sense he believes the Bible—as a Socinian, an Arian, or a Pelagian? Creeds not only have declared the faith of Christian communities but have served "to test and expose the character of dishonest men, who, under the plea of believers, entered the church to pollute its doctrine and to divide and scatter its members." Creeds then, as they should be now, were used against "the agents of the wicked one" who had crept into the church. "The orthodox creed was employed by the Church to correct the mischief by excluding the men."[12]

Stokes recognized that some people opposed the formulation of creeds. He believed that they were misled and confused two essentially different things, "the voluntary declaration of religious belief by Christian men, with the imposition of a creed by the civil magistrate." This misunderstanding has implicated "the liberty of the one act, in the appropriate condemnation of the other." What Christian would not be delighted to confess his faith to the world to set his witness in the open air and light for all to investigate? Those who have departed from the faith once delivered to the saints, with a few notable exceptions, maintain "an equivocal reserve" to make public such confession "under the pleas of adherence to the Scriptures." Stokes asked his readers to contrast the two ways.

> But who are most to be admired,—those who surround their profession with this mysterious reserve, and who in too many instances lead along an *unknown path* until it is too late to escape from the gloomy labyrinth? The advantages of an open-hearted honesty in a matter of such moment, are far too great to be bartered for the dry sentimentality of the Arian, or the frigid, genteel, but Christless morality of the Socinian party; and when it is remembered that our forefathers set the example with bonds, imprisonment, and death, as the penalty of their fidelity; surely it is not too much to expect that we rigidly adhere to a pattern so noble.[13]

Stokes wanted the confession of 1689 used as a foundation for Bible study. He wanted all Baptists "to make themselves thoroughly acquainted with the confession of 1689, by carefully examining the whole of its doctrines, with *every passage of Holy Scripture* which is adduced in their support." Later Stokes affirmed, "No human system of doctrines and precepts can be more scriptural than this, and none more expressive of the nature and design of the Lively Oracles." To reach that point of conviction, therefore Stokes recommended a thorough and systematic approach to the study.

> Let each member, laying his Bible before him, take the confession, statement by statement, paragraph by paragraph, and read seriously every passage of Scripture to which reference is made, and be earnest in seeking to know the mind of Christ in the words he is reading. This should not be done with haste, nor with a light and trifling spirit, but with seriousness, with gravity, and above all with fervent prayer for that blessed Spirit who "helpeth our infirmities." It should be done in the spirit of those who know they are living for eternity, and that above all other things it is necessary for them to understand what they are

about—what they are required to believe and obey—and how they are to act,—in order to have a solid confidence in the world to come. Every man is bound to know on what he is building his hope for eternal life, and to ascertain with precision, whether, what he takes for truth is really "the truth as it is in Jesus."[14]

When Alexander Campbell made war against Baptists as "tyrannical . . . in converting their own little confessions and covenants into creeds of excommunicating power and efficiency," many Baptists resented his insinuation that Baptists acted as medieval inquisitors by opposing his doctrine. Although some of the frontier Baptists showed less enthusiasm for the defining and disciplinary use of a confession than the older churches and associations in the east and southeast, they nevertheless enthusiastically embraced their usefulness for public witness. Affirming Scripture alone as the "bond of union and communion" and rejecting the label of creedalism, the editor of the *Western Baptist Review* still endorsed confessions as a lofty witness to truth. "Suffice it to say," the editor opined:

> that we know of nothing in the scriptures or in common sense, that requires the churches to be gagged, to prevent their proclaiming to the world, in this way, what they believe to be the great truths of our religion—that requires them to conceal their light under a bushel. And it is well known that churches, by publishing creeds, have stayed the injurious influences of slander and misrepresentation. . . . Indeed, unless a church is ashamed of her doctrine, we can see no good reason for her shrinking from its publication. Truth needs no concealment and seeks none. It seeks the light and the day. It shuns coverts and hiding-places, and stands on the mountain top to be seen and known of all men.[15]

S. M. Noel, a Kentucky colleague of the writer for the *Western Baptist Review* and more comprehensive in his affirmation of creeds, wrote on the subject of creeds in the circular letter for the Franklin Association in 1826. He proposed to answer the question, "Is it lawful and expedient, to adhere to a Creed, in the admission of members into the fellowship of the Church, and particularly in the admission of candidates into office?" Noel argued that any attempt to deny a religious society the use of a creed in determining its membership and officers "is a violent interference with the rights of conscience—it is tyranny."[16]

If a church takes no creed as a guide for the task of maintaining purity in teaching and membership, it forfeits its task to make a good confession and shine as lights in the world and opens itself to embrace into fellowship those whom the apostle anathematizes. If the adoption of a creed is an "unwarrantable exercise of power, the result is inevitable, that the Church is constrained to receive into her bosom, and cherish with her fellowship, those whom she must esteem her worst enemies; the enemies of truth."[17]

Noel, as others before him, rejected the argument that the use of a creed virtually declares that the Bible lacks clarity or is insufficient or is not infallible. No Protestant ever considered his confession as anything other than a human composition; it is rather an "epitome or summary exhibition of what the Scriptures teach." A creed qualifies itself in terms of Scripture; by definition it magnifies Scripture in expressing the mind's *credo* through the precise concerns and dominant ideas of Scripture. A Christian does not dishonor the Bible but does public homage to the Bible.

The Arian and Socinian profess to believe the Bible while they dishonor Christ. The Pelagian and semi-Pelagian make the same profession while they minimize the effects of sin and the necessity of the grace of God. The Sandemanian takes the Bible as his authority for defining faith in terms of mental assent to the historical truth of Christ's death and resurrection as reported by the apostles and virtually omitting the work of the Spirit. How can it dishonor Scripture for a Christian to say:

> I beg the privilege of declaring for myself, that while I believe with all my heart, that the Bible is the word of God, the only perfect rule of faith and manners, and the only ultimate test in all controversies; it plainly teaches as I read and believe, the deplorable and total depravity of human nature; the essential divinity of the Saviour; a trinity of persons in the Godhead; justification by the imputed righteousness of Christ; and regeneration and sanctification by the Holy Spirit, as indispensable to prepare the soul for Heaven. These I believe to be the radical truths, which God hath revealed in his word; and while they are denied by some, and frittered away, or perverted by others, who profess to believe that blessed word, I am verily persuaded, they are the fundamental principles, of the plan of salvation.[18]

A Dissenting Observation—but Only Apparently So

Some differences concerning confessions existed between Baptists in the North and South. Several, though by no means all, leaders of Baptist thinking in the North felt that the absence of a denominational confession of faith strengthened the doctrinal unity of Baptists. G. B. D. Pepper said, in 1876, "that there is no common symbol, no test of orthodoxy, no catechism, primer, body of Divinity, or hymn book—none of these so much as recommended by the denomination, much less adopted and authorized" in the end promotes "harmony, and powerfully tend[s] to unity of faith." Where freedom from coercion exists, heretics are free to leave, not forced to stay so as to corrupt the body. Where freedom exists, the evidence of the word alone convinces and gives life and thus creates the greatest possible unity.

"Wherever there is the truest, largest freedom, there men are in the best possible situation to learn and accept the truth, and so to agree," Pepper reasoned. "Convictions come of evidence," he continued, and "when real, only of evidence; and one is in position fairly to weigh evidence, only as he is free from compulsion."[19]

In spite of this characterization of noncreedal Baptist unity, Pepper recognized that all the attributes of confessionalism are present in Baptist doctrine and unity. He spoke of the doctrines held at the start of the century and "the life they begat was vigorous and earnest." This life as well as the doctrines arose from an experimental, rather than philosophical or speculative, knowledge of the teachings of Scripture. In addition, the doctrines so imbibed constituted the very life of the church. Of their own power they operated, "for the maintenance, of one particular kind of life, to the exclusion of every other, of one definite and distinct system of principle or doctrines, to the exclusion of all others."

In addition to the inherent logic of the ecclesiastical form Baptists embrace, Pepper said, "Closely related is the internal coherence of the faith, the unity of its constituents." That the various doctrines held by Baptists, here called "its constituents," have been seen as interrelated and necessarily coherent is indeed a "principal cause of denominational unity."[20]

Beyond that Pepper affirmed Baptist unity as secure because they had been kept "homogeneous to a great extent by homogeneous instruction." Their denominational literature, benevolent societies, preaching, and educational institutions have all contributed to "unify the denomination in a clearer, broader, more complete faith."[21]

Pepper surveyed the doctrines held in common by Baptists with other evangelicals as well as the doctrines that distinguish them. The deity and humanity of

Christ in one person, the mediatorship and sacrificial substitutionary redemptive work of Christ, and a Calvinistic understanding of the operations of grace all constitute essential doctrines for Baptists. Pepper explained:

> Finally, faith is the Holy Spirit's fruit. God calls it into exercise by his own efficient acting. It is, indeed, the sinner's own personal, rational act, conditioned by appropriate knowledge and mediated by appropriate motives, but the sacrifice of the sinful self is not product of the sinful self sacrificed. It is an act of one who is born of God, of the Spirit, from above. Squarely has the denomination asserted this, firmly believed it, earnestly maintained it. This supernatural element of faith involves the doctrine of Election. It presupposes that salvation is by God's own sovereign will, hence, by his own sovereign act. So have Baptists borne, and deserved to bear, the name of Calvinists, as holding in this capital doctrine with Calvin rather than with those who either co-ordinate the divine and the human, or condition God's acting on man's faith, and not man's faith of God's acting. Were Baptists to cease, thus far to be Calvinists, they would cease to be Baptists. . . . Baptists maintain it at their centre and circumference, and at every point intermediate.[22]

This kind of nonconfessionalism is a mere formality, for all the elements of confessional identity are abundantly present.

The same may be said for the way Francis Wayland (1796–1865) represented Baptist theology. When asked what creed the Baptists embrace, Wayland responded, "Our rule of faith and practice is the New Testament. We have no other authority to which we all profess submission."[23] The independence of the churches of Christ and the spiritual stewardship of each believer to read, explore, and understand Scripture for himself combine to render the external imposition of a creed anomalous to the ecclesiology of Baptists. In fact, Wayland confidently asserted, "This very absence of any established creed is in itself the cause of our unity."[24]

Several factors show that Wayland did not indulge a principle opposed to an individual, a church, or an association publishing a confession of faith. First, he recognized that common belief in churches validly resulted in public confession. "If several churches," he speculated, "understand the Scriptures in the same way, and all unite in the same confession, then this expresses the opinions and belief of those who profess it." Then, to reinforce the populist nature of the confession, he added, "It, however, expresses their belief, because all of them, from the study of the

Scriptures, understand them in the same manner; and not because any tribunal has imposed such interpretations upon them."[25]

Next, the clarity of Scripture leads necessarily to Christian agreement on its teachings in a large number of specific areas of doctrine. An inspired record of pure truth brings earnest believers under its constant influence ever nearer to one another in their understanding and expressions of truth. "The nearer the opinions of men approach to its teachings, the nearer they approach to each other." This way of reaching truth and unity is "adapted to the nature of man as an intelligent and accountable being" and is a "solid and definite basis of unity."

Moreover, Wayland noted that the present doctrinal position of Baptist churches differed little from what it had always been. His statement assumed knowledge of the confessions of the first generation of modern Baptists. "I do not believe that any denomination of Christians exists," he claimed, "which, for so long a period as the Baptists, have maintained so invariably the truth of their early confessions." This is demonstrated by the fact that "the confessions of the persecuted Baptists . . . are almost identical with those of our churches of the present day in this country." Though he guessed that "not one in ten thousand of our members ever heard of their existence" (meaning the existence of the early confessions), he demonstrated that the vocabulary of those confessions has been maintained through the centuries.

Finally, Wayland discussed theological continuity and change in Baptist life in terms of confessional categories. He began with the Trinity and the person of Christ, discussed the creation of man in innocence, his fall into sin, the nature of the law, salvation by grace alone, and disagreements over the extent of the atonement. He affirmed that Baptists believe that God "in infinite mercy, has elected some to everlasting life," and that the Spirit operates effectually to bring them to "salvation and sanctification."[26]

Both Pepper and Wayland, therefore, saw Baptists as resistant to the imposition of a creed from civil or ecclesiastical authorities upon a church. They did not find a church's, or an association's, adoption of a confession irregular if it arose from the common life of the church or association and the personal study and understanding of Scripture. We also should note carefully that they were highly pleased with the degree of doctrinal unity of Baptists at the midpoint of the nineteenth century. Both gave tacit recognition of the powerful and positive influence of the early confessional life of Baptists.

Pepper and Wayland also recognized that substantial doctrinal divergence would result in discipline, or failing that, deterioration of the Baptist witness. "The belief in baptism by immersion may be entertained by a man of almost any persuasion, but this alone does not unite him with us," Wayland observed. In order to seal this point that doctrinal identity mattered greatly, he continued, "Our churches, with one accord, always and everywhere, have held Unitarianism to be a grave and radical error."[27]

Baptist doctrinal commitments, therefore, go far beyond the mere acceptance of our distinctive view of one of the ordinances. Such commitments require, even for Pepper and Wayland, a larger and more encyclopedic grasp of biblical truth, clearly articulated for the agreement of all. Had either of these men observed in the mid-nineteenth century a phenomenon that became common in the twentieth, their argument, I believe, would have changed significantly. Had they seen many people claiming to be Baptists while rejecting the historic confessional doctrines of Baptists, and appealing to individual responsibility and freedom as the sole justification for their retaining the name "Baptist," their alarm would have driven them to an invocation of defining doctrines as enunciated in the historic Baptist confessions.

The Creedal Status of Confessions

J. P. Boyce (1827–1888) attended Brown University while Wayland was president. Wayland exerted great influence on Boyce's view of educational theory. As a corrective to Wayland, however, Boyce more boldly advocated the use of creeds in Baptist life. In his inaugural address as professor of theology at Furman University (1856), he defended their use at every level of Baptist life from church to denominational institution. A clear declaration of faith appropriate to the necessity of each case must be forthcoming as it is required by the biblical mandate of confessing with the mouth that Jesus is Lord.

For the theological professor, Boyce recommended the Charleston Association Confession of Faith since it represented the theology of all of the Baptist churches in South Carolina. "Let that then be adopted, and let subscription to it on the part of each theological professor be required as an assurance of his entire agreement with its views of doctrine and of his determination to teach fully the truth which it expresses and nothing contrary to its declarations."[28] The adoption of such a principle as recommended by Boyce on this occasion would mark the existence of a reformation of the most thorough and God-centered sort.

Fullness in a confession of faith, however, should not inhibit the reception of new converts into church membership. A credible testimony of a saving work of grace gives babes in Christ joyful entrée to the community of believers. The minimum of truth couched within a credible conversion testimony, however, does not suffice for the standard to which the babe should grow or as a guide for the teaching ministry of a church. As B. H. Carroll (1843–1914) said, "The minimum of entrance qualification into the church can never be made the limit of the church creed, and especially cannot be made the limit of examination for ordination to the ministry."[29]

Associations adopted confessions and expected their member churches to abide by the truth expressed in these expressions, openly to propagate it through preaching and teaching, and joyfully to conform to its expressions and its implications as long as they maintained the association's fellowship. Denominational structures have flourished or faltered in proportion to their willingness to give open adherence to a healthy confession of faith. An unwillingness to confess a body of definite truth often betrays a spiritual sickness unto death already at work. J. B. Gambrell (1841–1921) indicated that a destructive attitude lurked behind resistance to creeds. "The cry against creeds is lacking in sound judgment," Gambrell wrote, and it "comes from those who wish to evaporate religious thoughts into theological mist." Opposers of creeds "wish all the fences pulled down and everything unsettled."[30]

A true reformation must recapture the willingness as well as the *historical and biblical aptitude* to embrace a strong confession of faith. While the idea of doctrinal integrity and confessional fidelity has been given some thought and has played an important role in certain aspects of the beginnings of reformation, the implications of giving serious attention to the full range of doctrines in the confessions remains to be explored. If we only recapture the symbolic idea that confessions are important and represent a willingness to be stewards of the mysteries of God but fail to deliver faithfulness to the particular articles contained in the confessions, we invite theological decline and spiritual ineffectiveness. Again Carroll expressed with power and clarity the ultimate goal of confessing Christianity.

> A Christian's creed should enlarge, and not diminish, up to the last utterance of revelation in order that each article might be transmitted into experience.
>
> A church with a little creed is a church with a little life. The more doctrines a church can agree on, the greater its power, and the wider its usefulness. The fewer its articles of faith, the fewer its bonds of union and compactness.

The modern cry: "Less creed and more liberty," is a degeneration from the vertebrate to the jellyfish, and means less unity and less morality, and it means more heresy—Definitive truth does not create heresy—it only exposes and corrects. Shut off the creed and the Christian world would fill up with heresy unsuspected and uncorrected, but none the less deadly.

. . .

This body of truth, constituting the creed of the church, is held as of inestimable value, and was ready to pronounce anathema against an angel from heaven who would preach any other gospel. It is a radical mistake to say that these New Testament articles of faith were few and simple. They touched, among other things, the nature, being, attributes, and offices of the triune God; the Holy inspired Scriptures, the church with its polity, terms of membership, officers, ordinances, and mission; the whole plan of salvation from election, foreordination, and predestination to glorification; the family; the citizen, the whole of this life, and the whole of the life to come; the ministry of angels good and the opposition of angels bad; and the final judgment.

Particularly they touched the personality of the Messiah, his pre-existence and deity, his emptying himself of his heavenly glory and prerogatives to assume in his first advent the body of his humiliation, in order to [work] his vicarious expiation of sin on the cross, his going in his spirit after death to make the atonement in the holy of holies; his second advent to earth in order to assume his body of glorification, and his ascension and exaltation to the throne of the universe as a royal priest; his sending of his vicar, or vicegerent, the Holy Spirit, to accredit, infill, endue with power, and to abide with his church on earth; his third advent to assume his mystical body, the glorified church, to raise the dead and judge the world.

Broad as is the forgoing statement, it does not include all the clearly defined articles of the New Testament faith. . . .

Very solemnly I would warn the reader against any teaching that decries doctrines, or which would reduce the creed of the church into two or three articles.[31]

Reformation and confession cannot be separated.

Chapter 3

Priority and Power of Truth in Proclamation

Irreducibly Important

The church is built by the Word. God has chosen to save his people through the task, for the most part, of preaching. Many people come to Christ through personal reading of Scripture, through the individual witness of others, but the appointed task of the church for the calling out of the people is preaching. Paul knew that his calling involved the proclamation of the Word (Titus 1:3). He wrote to the Romans that God would establish them "according to my gospel and the preaching of Jesus Christ" (Rom. 16:25). "How shall they hear without a preacher? And how shall they preach unless they are sent?" he asked as he defended justification by faith (Rom. 10:14–15 NKJV). "We preach Christ crucified" he reminded the Corinthians (1 Cor. 1:23), a message that though foolish to the Greeks was the power of God. He reminded both the Corinthians and the Romans of the message, the gospel, that he "preached" to them.

Paul told the Galatians that the gospel "which was preached by me is not according to man" (Gal. 1:11). God had set him apart even from before his birth, and called him by grace "that I might preach Him among the Gentiles" (Gal. 1:16). His exposition of the mystery of grace to the Gentiles culminated in this marvel that "to me, the very least of all saints, this grace was given, to preach to the Gentiles the unfathomable riches of Christ" (Eph. 3:8). He passed this task along with a note of urgency to Timothy, "Preach the word" (2 Tim. 4:2).

Tell the Truth

These urgings to preach take for granted that the content of proclamation is truth. Some might preach "another gospel" which is no gospel at all; it will bring condemnation. No amount of zeal or earnestness to prompt sinners to commit to the message will transform error into truth (Gal. 1:7–9). On the other hand, some might preach with impure motivation, but as long as their message is true, Paul rejoiced (Phil. 1:15–18). When he preached to the Thessalonians, Paul reminded them that God's choice of them to salvation involved belief in the truth; conversely, those deceived by Satan did not love truth but believed a lie (2 Thess. 2:10–11, 14). Paul treated as synonymous the "gospel" and "truth" when he reminded the Ephesians that their sealing with the Holy Spirit was on the occasion of their "listening to the message of truth, the gospel of your salvation" (Eph. 1:13).

Peter identified the initial evidence of the new birth as "obedience to the truth" (1 Pet. 1:22). The new birth involves much more but can certainly include no less. John distinguished between genuine Christianity and heretical teaching, using the categories "spirit of truth" and "spirit of error" (1 John 4:6). The requirement God had of Job's aggravating friends is interesting. He specified sacrifices for them because they had spoken about God *what was not right*. God's wrath was kindled against them, and he threatened to deal with them according to their folly for their having given such passionate theological expositions in error (Job 42:7–9).

The insistence on truth, revealed truth, counteracts a whole life lived under the power of delusion. An entire worldview built on error and nurtured by the desires of the flesh does not fall easily. Clearly nothing less than divine power works to rescue unbelievers from the power of darkness (Col. 1:13; Eph. 1:19). This divine power, however, operates within the realm of truth. The mind is convinced of its reality, and the heart embraces its beauty under the regenerating power of the Spirit. He is the Spirit of truth. The messenger, therefore, must place utter confidence in its proclamation, "not walking in craftiness or adulterating the word of God, but by the manifestation of truth" working to pierce the conscience (2 Cor. 4:2).

Word and Spirit

The undiluted and dynamic consistency and sympathy of revealed truth with the powerful and immediate operations of the divine Spirit teased from Robert Hall Jr. (1764–1831) a compelling defense of truth as the only medium in which the preacher should traffic. The final triumph of the truth of the gospel, Hall argued convincingly, receives absolute certainty from the efficacious operations of the Spirit as "a standing ordinance of heaven." A minister of Christ does not rest his success "on the force of moral suasion." The Lord opens the heart, and the Lord gives the increase.

The work of the Spirit, however, in no way dissipates the preacher's obligation to present truth with the confidence that truth saves. Remaining unconvinced of this in all its attendant connections disturbs the seriousness, tenderness, and majesty that should characterize his addresses and leaves the preacher open to "amusing speculations, or unprofitable novelties." That the giving of the Spirit, however, is connected with "the publication of an external revelation" and that he sets his seal only "to the testimony of Jesus" should intercept any "enthusiastic pretension, by leaving the appeal to scripture as full and uncontrolled as if no such agency were supposed." Hall enforced his thought with further explanation of the relation of Word and Spirit.

> The idea of his immediate interposition must necessarily increase our veneration for whatever is connected with it; and let it ever be remembered, that the internal illumination of the Spirit is merely intended to qualify the mind for distinctly perceiving, and cordially embracing those objects, and no other, which are exhibited in the written word. To dispel prejudice, to excite a disposition for inquiry, and to infuse that love of the truth, without which we can neither be transformed by its power nor bow to its dictates, is the grand scope of spiritual agency; and how this should derogate from the dignity of the truth itself, it is not easy to conceive. The inseparable alliance between the Spirit and the Word, secures the harmony of the divine dispensations; and since that spirit of truth can never contradict himself, whatever impulse he may give, whatever disposition he may communicate, it involves no irreverence towards that divine agent to compare his operations with that standing revelation, which, equally claiming him for its author, he has expressly appointed for the trial of the spirits.[1]

Basil Manly Jr. (1825–1892) approved of Hall's representation and embraced it as his own. The inseparability of truth and Spirit for gospel efficacy provides the only foundation of hope for the gospel worker. Reviewing the human situation in itself, Manly confronted the apparent impossibility of the task of winning souls. He painted a distressing picture of the seemingly invincible obnoxiousness of sinful human nature.

> We have to overcome entire indifference. The souls that are to be won care nothing for spiritual blessings, having lost, through the fall, the right sense of such things. We are proposing to make those serious who have given all their days to levity and amusement, and those spiritual, who have been entirely engrossed in worldly care. . . . But we have to encounter the hostility of the heart, and not its indifference and reluctance merely. We have, as our first business, to fasten the charge of guilt upon men; to make them not only acknowledge, but feel their utter sinfulness and degradation in God's sight; to produce a sense of condemnation and self-abhorrence, where self-complacency had filled the mind, and love of pleasure ruled the life. Our efforts are opposed by the passions of men, too, as well as by their pride. Sins dear as a right eye must be renounced, and evil habits cherished as the right hand, must be cut off. The interests also of men, as regards this life, are frequently opposed to our errand. Gainful, as well as pleasurable sins, must be abandoned. In fact, the whole nature must be changed. Our effort is nothing less than to win a wholly perverted and depraved soul back to purity, and fit it for dwelling with God.[2]

What means will overcome such impervious unconcern and hostility? Manly suggested that "the instrumentality proposed, is the truth of God, made effective by the Spirit of God." So deeply wrought and so deeply and thoroughly evil is man's disaster that only divine enlightenment produced by the same divine energy that raised Christ from the dead can suffice for the task. But the Spirit is the Spirit of truth, and that by which he operates upon reasonable volitional beings is that which in its nature has the tendency to convince and change. Without contradiction, truth must be wielded as a two-edged sword.

> The truth! What more adapted to move a reasonable being than reason? What more likely to convince and change him than the truth?

No truth is powerless or unimportant; but what sort of truth is this? The truth of God, the truth that comes from God and leads to God, the truth concerning himself and his law, his promises and designs, the truth as it is in Jesus. All truth elevates, but this sanctifies; all truth benefits, but this is able to save the souls; all truth makes men wiser, but this makes them wise unto salvation.[3]

Strong Medicine for Deadly Infection

Truth must be preached fully, saturatingly, unrelentingly, without compromise, from beginning to end through argument, illustrations, conclusions, and applications. The hearer, believer or unbeliever, must never get any relief from the bombardment of truth. The amount of misinformation and false pleasures trumpeted by the prince of the power of the air pours down unremittingly from the world system on the Christian. He is pummeled with error, tantalized with lust, baited by power, assaulted by worldly glamour, and molded by an amoral system mercilessly opposed to righteousness. Christian holiness built on an absolute standard of righteousness appears to the world as a judgmental, hateful, venomous kind of hypocrisy. He must cope in a world that glorifies and rewards self-centeredness, repression, and hate.

The believer's only opportunity to hear an argument mounted against the torrent of temporality pressed daily and hourly into his consciousness comes when a Christian minister stands to preach the Word of God. Will he hear anything that challenges and strips bare the lies that have been pressed on him from every quarter? Or will he hear a few assertions from a biblical text surrounded by warm stories garnished with the trappings of sentimentality and never enter substantially into the truth? Will he be called on without doctrinal instruction to pull himself together and get with it for Christ, decide to do right, and make Christ the center of his life?

Sometimes biblical words and phrases can be used like charms, with an aura of magic and power but void of reasonable explanation. Christian truth does not function that way. Christians cannot be made strong that way. The real effects of Christ's humiliation and exaltation, unfolded into the conscience by powerful and faithful biblical exposition, will bare the soul before God and empty the world of its false and destructive charm.

Will a desperately thirsty believer be oppressed as an unspiritual person and be sent to the dry well of the so-called "Spirit-filled life" formula and yet never be taught the powerful truths of the sanctifying work, gifts, and fruit of the Spirit already operative in him through Christ? Can he wrestle against the dark forces of spiritual wickedness without substantial instruction in the truth as it is in Jesus and the wisdom that allows him to "appraise all things" (1 Cor. 2:15)? Can he stand firm unless he has his loins girded with truth (Eph. 6:10–17)? The world is filled with life-sapping lies. Biblical truth is the sure antidote.

Does Inerrancy Guarantee Biblical Preaching?

The recovery of biblical inerrancy would seem naturally to imply that biblical truth pulsates at the center and through the extremities of every message and gives life to the sermon from beginning to end. By God's grace, serious calls for a reform of preaching and excellent examples of doctrinally informed exposition ring clearly in influential pockets of worldwide Baptist life. Though some voices call for less preaching and more "art, dance and music,"[4] men of rare talent and conviction dot the Baptist landscape. Other evangelical denominations have a positive influence on Baptist circles. These facts give hope that seriousness about preaching may yet prevail. In the theologically recovering Southern Baptist Convention, expository preaching is being given prominence in the theological seminary curriculums. The concept looms large as a *desideratum,* and a growing number of graduates pursue the practice seriously.

In the warmth of these encouragements, however, sufficient cause for deep concern still reverberates from Sunday to Sunday in Baptist pulpits. Serious text-driven, truth-saturated preaching may be heard only by listening carefully. A non-inerrantist described expository preaching pejoratively: "You tie a Scripture to a chair and beat it with a rubber hose for 20 minutes to see what you can get out of it."[5] One may not expect much in the way of truth-centered exposition from a preacher with such a perspective on exposition. Though inerrantists have a better theory about biblical authority, sermons of biblical substance pop up much less frequently than needed. They come as refreshing interludes to give relief to the droning run-on sentence of mesmerizing emptiness in much that passes for preaching. Perhaps more solid, biblically faithful exposition is the intent, but often it is not the fact.

Unbelievers who need the challenge of truth and believers who are hungry for meat are given cream-filled sponge cake. Minds and hearts undernourished and in need of the meat starve while scratching the sermon for some food. Needing an engaged exposition that sustains a critical inquiry into the text throughout the sermon while setting the text in the framework of biblical theology, they hear a repetition of four or five favorite ideas without any connection with the text.

Believers, dependent on the objective truths of biblical revelation, hear many a sermon whose substance arises from an existential impression reported by the preacher of what God instructed him to say. This method of sermon preparation cuts short the task of faithful exposition. Tragically common, this phenomenon appears under a formula similar to this: "As I was praying about this message and looking at this text, the Lord spoke to my heart. He wants me to tell you . . ." Most often follows a cleverly worded but theologically vacuous point that has little to do with the text and often is out of harmony, or at best indifferent to, an integrated biblical theology of the idea.

The motive of this approach is to arrest the hearers with some word that appears fresh and peculiarly designed by God for them at that moment. The urgency of perceived existential relevance overwhelms the importance of the eternal interest and at the same time destroys the kind of freshness that engages the mind in an unending fascination with life-giving truth. Robert Hall eloquently described the power of textual simplicity and biblical faithfulness.

To a serious mind, the truths of the christian [sic] religion appear with such an air of unaffected greatness, that, in comparison of these, all other speculations and reasonings seem like the amusements of childhood. When the Deity, the incarnation, the atonement, the resurrection of the Son of God, the sanctification of the church, and the prospects of glory, have engaged our contemplation, we feel, in turning our attention to other objects, a strange descent, and perceive, with the certainty of demonstration, that, as the earth is too narrow for the full developement [sic] of these mysteries, they are destined by their consequences and effects, to impregnate an eternal duration. . . . Are you desirous of fixing the attention of your hearers strongly on their everlasting concerns? No peculiar refinement of thought, no subtlety of reasoning, much less the pompous exaggerations of secular eloquence, are wanted for that purpose: you have only to imbibe deeply the mind of Christ, to let his doctrine enlighten, his love inspire your heart, and your situation, in comparison of other speakers, will resemble that of the angel of the apocalypse, who was seen standing in the sun. Draw your instructions immediately from the Bible; the more immediately they are derived from that source, and the less they are tinctured with human distinctions and refinements, the more salutary, and the more efficacious. Let them be taken fresh from the spring.[6]

For Hall, freshness and relevance arise from one's engagement with the biblical text, not from a personal inspiration above the text, beyond the text, parallel to the text, inspired by the text, or unrelated to the text.

A strategically influential pastor, laying claim to a freshness unlike that which Hall proposed, received "fresh fire from the altar" in contemplating the text of Isaiah 6. How many of God's sheep have been led to endure this kind of pompous imposition! He never read the text to the congregation, for it was not apparent that its content was germane to his sermon. All of his points supposedly flew straight from the altar from which were drawn the coals that cleansed Isaiah's lips. Oh, that such had been the case, for then the entire sermon probably would never have assaulted a Christian pulpit. Each succeeding assertion came as a result of an immediate perception of what God wanted him to say to that particular congregation (and several others before whom he had preached the same sermon).

Some of his ideas rescued his hearers from mistakes they might have derived from Scripture. He informed the congregation, for example, that the idea that people were not searching for God was a false idea. He claimed to be able to demonstrate this on any platform in the world and proceeded to massage his point by telling the story of an affluent but frustrated woman whose life was falling apart and who prayed that God would send someone to help her put it back together. Then he, the preacher, showed up at her door. Point proved. A sentimental story supposedly overcomes centuries of serious interaction with the biblical doctrine of total depravity. And beyond that the sermon made no serious attempt at any biblical exposition.

Every minister must avoid the temptation to substitute cleverness for faithfulness. Though no scientific survey could measure the tendency, one receives the distinct impression from hearing large numbers of sermons from a variety of pulpiteers who have the ears of large numbers of congregants and media listeners that the urge for novelty and uniqueness often overwhelms them. Outline and alliteration frequently determine content more that text. Anecdote and speculative observation steer doctrine and application away from truth and into an alley obscured with the uncertainties of the preacher's personal insight. Forgetting that it is required of a steward that he be found faithful, the preacher's style or personal charisma gradually press their way to the forefront.

Robert Hall anticipated this tendency and stated the case with arresting sobriety. "A doctrine, full, pure, perfect, to which nothing can be added without debasing its spirit, nothing taken away without impairing its proportions, is committed to our trust," Hall reminded James Robertson. It should be "retained and preserved, just as we have received it, and delivered to our hearers in all its primitive simplicity."[7]

The Detraction of Illustration

Even in messages, however, in which the work of study has been done, the theory of communication reduces to a precious minimum the time given to theological interaction. The power of truth gives way to warm personal illustrations that are supposed to unlock the secrets of each point of the exposition. Apparently, so goes the theory, if the congregation identifies with the personality of the speaker, his message immediately becomes more credible and engaging. In fact, much precious teaching time for the truth is lost. A false impression of both the content and purpose of the Bible gains ascendancy over the basic assumption of the transforming power of truth.

A Bible conference speaker, prominent in theological education, asserted, in opposition to the spirit of Diotrephes (3 John 9) that Christ alone is preeminent. Now is the time for a presentation of biblical teachings on the person of Christ as God/man, his infinite worthiness as uniquely qualified Savior, his continual enjoyment of the unbroken love of his Father, his right to judge all flesh, and the consequent irrational, sinful haughtiness of any sinful mortal injecting a personal agenda as of greater concern than the truth of Christ.

This theological idea aborts, however, under the scalpel of a lengthy and humorous illustration about the speaker's college life and his failed attempts at humility. Did he miss the opportunity for an exposition of the infinite superiority of the person of Christ? Did his feverish attachment to personal illustrations rob Christ of his glory? Absolutely. The speaker forfeited the ministry's birthright of serious engagement with revealed truth. Consequently, his self-exhibiting words bordered on idolatry in sidestepping a discussion of the preeminence of the glories of Christ.

John A. Broadus (1827–1895) wrote of this danger in the careless use of illustrations. In the closing section of an excellent discussion of illustration in the sermon, Broadus warned, "Carefully avoid turning attention away from the subject illustrated to the illustration itself. This is obviously a very grave fault, but it is often committed." He continued, "So many hearers are caring mainly for entertainment, that it is a sad thing if we divert their minds from some subject they ought to consider, to the curious or admiring examination of the mere apparatus by which we throw light on it."[8]

Charles Spurgeon (1834–1892) pointed to the urgency of truth-speaking in the preaching ministry. The men of his Pastor's College heard him speak in one of their Friday sessions on the subject, "On Conversion as Our Aim." In his first point he urged his students "to preach most prominently those truths which are likely to lead to this end." He spoke shortly but saltily on several key doctrines: Christ and him crucified, the evil of sin, the depravity of human nature, the necessity of the Holy Spirit's divine operations, the certainty that every transgression will be punished, the "soul-saving doctrine" of a "real bona fide substitutionary sacrifice," justification by faith, the boundless mercy of God as seen "in calm consistency with stern justice and unlimited sovereignty."[9] Most conducive to conversion in Spurgeon's view of things are those doctrines most maligned by many others.

> Men must be told that they are dead, and that only the Holy Spirit can quicken them; that the Spirit works according to his own good pleasure, and that no man can claim his visitations or deserve his aid. This is thought to be very discouraging teaching, and it is, but men need to be discouraged when they are seeking salvation in a wrong manner. To put them out of conceit of their own abilities is a great help toward bringing them to look out of self to another, even the Lord Jesus. The doctrine of election and other great truths which declare salvation to be all of grace, and to be not the right of the creature, but the gift of the Sovereign Lord, are all calculated to hide pride from man, and so to prepare him to receive the mercy of God.[10]

Conclusion

Pulpit power exerted the single most formative impact on Baptist identity. From Keach, Bunyan, Gill, Fuller, Hall, and Spurgeon to Furman, Manly, Fuller, Mell, Boyce, and Broadus, the ministry of proclamation had its biblically sanctioned effect. Baptists grew numerous in churches, maintained gospel purity, and had strong theological convictions at the popular level. Without a recovery of confidence in the transforming power of proclaimed truth, the reformation will fail, and the Baptist advance for truth and the divine glory will stagnate and corrupt.

Confidence must not be delusive, however, which it often is when taking the form of certainty without reality. Rigorous self-criticism and examination must continue to drive the pulpit ministry to preach not ourselves but Christ as Lord, to preach Christ and him crucified, not to handle the Word of God deceitfully, to make clear manifestation of the truth, and that when our mouths are opened, to make known the mystery of the gospel.

Chapter 4

Baptists Must Recover the Work of Evangelism, Part I

Introduction

Because of the importance of evangelism from both a practical and doctrinal standpoint, and because of the congenital sense of identity Baptists have with it, this chapter will have two parts. The Gospel narratives, the historical accounts of Acts, and the intensely constructed doctrine in the Epistles show evangelism to be a "work." Of course, we are not speaking of a meritorious work or a work of righteousness on our part. By work we mean a progressive, sustained, and deliberate activity that assumes some orderly arrangement of materials in a purposeful, knowledgeable manner.

A work of evangelism, on the part of the evangelist, involves a knowledge of the work of Christ, the work of the Spirit, the nature of the efficacy of the Word of God, and the operations of the human soul under a work of conviction, new birth, repentance, and faith. The generations that fabricated Baptist ecclesiology from its biblical raw materials used gold, jewels, and precious stones as they worked with discernment from a necessary and vital knowledge of the fountain of human decision and the conditions and evidences of a work of God's Spirit.

The Danger of a Corrupted Evangelism

Biblical evangelism cannot be severed from the proclamation of truth. The connection is vital. Sever and die. Ironically, a major factor in the decline of Baptist identity has been the zealous practice of a redefined evangelism. Clearly, zeal may be good or bad depending on the cause to which it is devoted. When devoted to evangelism, it is good; but when the evangelism to which it is devoted takes short-cuts around the gospel, zeal may be a catalyst for theological dissolution. The coincidence of evangelistic minimalism and encroaching modernism in the late nineteenth and early twentieth centuries made strange bedfellows for theological deconstruction. Renewal in the work of evangelism involves a cordial embracing of full-orbed theology as friendly to, not destructive of, evangelism, along with a purposeful execution of a theology of means—or the methods ordered by God for the effectual operation of his gospel message.

The ideal of a regenerate church membership has forced Baptists to depend on conversion growth for the perpetuity of their churches. Neither magisterial support nor infant baptism and membership have had any hand in the origin and growth of Baptists. The children of pious Baptists, though loved, cherished, taught, catechised, and nurtured, have historically been seen as children of wrath and in need of converting grace. Evangelism within and without has been the life-blood of Baptist churches and will continue to be if they survive.

A substantial shift in both the theology and methodology of evangelism has occurred, however, and threatens the concept of the regenerate church just as surely as the doctrine of infant baptism. A method of evangelism built on a redefinition of regeneration may produce exactly the kind of carnal membership in churches to which Baptist ecclesiology is hostile. In this approach the "work" of evangelism declines under the pressure of an "act" of evangelism.

The Biblical Components of Evangelism

In 2 Timothy the "work" of an evangelist should be seen in light of Paul's allusions to that work throughout the book and indeed. throughout his ministry, Paul endured "all things for the sake of those who are chosen" (2 Tim. 2:10), thus summarizing the years of his unremitting suffering as the Apostle to the Gentiles. He told Timothy to continue in the things that he had *learned* and become *convinced* of because he knew from whom he had learned them and that the holy Scriptures were able to make a person wise unto salvation. Timothy's conversion came as a result of consistent acquaintance with the Scriptures argued so cogently that he became "convinced" of their truthfulness. Through them he became "wise unto salvation" (2 Tim. 3:15 KJV).

Paul's method of proclamation consisted of reasoning and persuading his hearers that Jesus was the Christ. The work of Paul described in Acts 13–14 at Antioch, Iconium, Lystra, and Derbe involved intense biblical preaching. This included extended rational discourse on the grounds of Scripture in an effort to convince his hearers of the truth of the message. When grasped with the heart, the believer enters a pilgrimage with the recognition that "through many tribulations we must enter the kingdom of God" (Acts 14:22). They spoke "boldly" and "continued to preach the gospel" (Acts 14:7). When inquirers followed them, they "were urging them to continue in the grace of God" (Acts 13:43). At Iconium, in the face of organized opposition, Paul and his cohort "spent a long time . . . speaking boldly with reliance upon the Lord" (14:3). From Paul's inscripted version of his preaching, we learn that this included detailed instruction concerning justification, the use of the law, atonement, sanctification, and other doctrines.

We also learn that true faith involves the acceptance and submission to doctrinal propositions. Falling away from those truths is an indication that a person does not have true faith (1 Cor. 12:3; 15:1–2; Gal. 3:1–4 with the doctrinal exposition that follows; Phil. 3:17–19; Col. 1:21–23). Careful instruction as a part of, as well as a complement to, bold proclamation constituted Paul's evangelism. He commended this kind of evangelism in Epaphras when he described the conversion of the Colossian Christians.

> We always give thanks to God, Father of our Lord Jesus Christ, when we pray for you. This is because we heard of your faith in Christ Jesus and the love that you have for all the saints based on the hope laid by for you in heaven. This is what you heard before in the word of truth, the gospel that has come to you. Even as in all the world also it is constantly bearing fruit and increasing, so also among you. This has been happening since the day you heard and came to know with fullness the grace of God in truth. You learned it just so from Epaphras,

our beloved fellow bond-servant, who is a faithful servant of Christ on our behalf. (Col. 1:3–7, author's translation)

Paul used phrases such as "faith, love, and hope"—all of which point to a full display of truth as Epaphras preached the gospel to them. This is the content that they had believed and, hopefully, embraced with the heart. This particular gospel, as preached to them by Epaphras, was the one that had established faith, love, and hope wherever it had gone in the world and would do the same among them. The Colossians heard and came to know with fullness the grace of God in truth. This truth, when written on the heart by the Spirit, that is in "all spiritual wisdom and understanding" (Col. 1:9), grants a harvest of good work and continually increasing knowledge of God. This particular gospel, however, and not the false views of the gnostics, alone bears this fruit of goodness and knowledge. The evangelism of Epaphras had been thorough and passionately doctrinal.

Health and Sickness

When viewed in all its connections, evangelism is the most urgent and intensely practical manifestation of Christian theology. Every category of systematic theology has a direct bearing on evangelism, both its matter and its manner. The historical interplay between evangelism and theology is complicated, sometimes theology driving evangelism and sometimes evangelism driving and altering theology.

The earliest Particular Baptists and General Baptists saw a vital connection between conviction of sin and the call to faith. Doctrinally informed urgency about salvation drove early Baptists such as Thomas Helwys, John Spilsbury, Benjamin Keach, Dan Taylor, and others into a doctrine-centered evangelism. Conviction of sin must be personal, and it must be related to gospel issues as well as law issues, or else faith in Christ makes no sense and amounts to mere cant. Hanserd Knollys contended that an element of true conviction involved the sinner's awareness of "piersing Christ, sleighting Gods offer of him to you upon Gospel-tearmes, and dispising him, though tendered in a Covenant of grace." A convicted sinner will sense that he has "abused, sleighted, and neglected free mercy and rich grace [and] stood out against God, preferred the world, and the things of this life, yea my owne base sinfull lusts before Jesus Christ."[1]

Both the General Baptists and the Particular Baptists, however, managed their distinctive doctrines in such a way as to damage evangelism. The theological Achilles' heel of Arminianism lies in its tendency to minimize the impact of sin on the will. This in turn realigns the relation between the divine and the human in salvation; this realignment, sadly, has often led to a diminished estimation of the character of the Redeemer and of course a reconceptualization of the nature of evangelism. Particular Baptists isolated the implosive energy in their doctrines of sin and sovereignty in such a way that they argued that not only an awareness of sin but an awareness of the effectual working of the Spirit necessarily preceded a sinner's warrant to go to Christ for salvation. Doctrines concerning both the deity and humanity of Christ, the effects of original sin, and a substitutionary atonement suffered under the General Baptists. On the other hand, some ministers among the Particular Baptists lost confidence in any way to issue a universally valid call to repentance from sin and faith in Christ.

From Knollys to Keach, orthodox doctrine and the universal urgency of gospel preaching remained in a state of healthy integration. Truth and evangelistic warmth embraced each other as friends of the utmost compatibility but without any pressure for transactional, or decisionistic, evangelism. The eighteenth century saw conflict among the Particular Baptists as some began to deny that universal calls could coexist with total depravity and the exclusive sovereignty of God in salvation. John Brine (1703–1765) said that it can't be proved that Jesus ever asserted evangelical repentance to be the "duty of unregenerate Persons." It becomes their duty when "they have warrant from the divine Word, to consider God as their Redeemer in Christ, which no unregenerate Men have any Warrant to do."[2] Only those assured that they are regenerate and are the subjects of God's eternal determination to save have any warrant for faith in Christ. This position constitutes a radical shift in theological definition and practical emphasis.

A Key to Recovery

A new urgency in the evangelism mandate for Christians was reflected in the theological breakthroughs indicated by the title of Andrew Fuller's great work *The Gospel Worthy of All Acceptation* (1785). His struggle with hyper-Calvinism, "False Calvinism" as he called it, caused him great grief. He concluded that it "enervates every part of vital godliness."[3] Though he shared their belief in the "necessity of an almighty work of God the Spirit, to new model the whole soul, to form in us new principles or dispositions," he also believed that "free and solemn addresses, invitations, calls and warnings to [the lost] to be not only consistent, but directly adapted, as means, in the hand of the Spirit of God, to bring them to Christ."[4]

Fuller's work reflected a revival of the theology of means. Baptists and other evangelicals on both sides of the Atlantic gave marvelous mental energy to analyzing the correlation between depravity, grace, truth, calling, the work of the Spirit, and the relation between the eternal decree of predestination and the temporal disposition of those decrees through obedience to divine revelation. In a sermon entitled "The Universal Spread of the Gospel," Andrew Broaddus (1770–1848) expressed his amused bewilderment at some of his brethren. They prayed earnestly for the spread of the blessed gospel throughout the entire world that it might be filled with the knowledge of God and then opposed missionary operations as man's invention "calculated to rob God of his honor, by taking the work out of his hands." Their complaint might have been just and their zeal honorable if God were disposed to make such knowledge universal without the preaching of the gospel or the use of any means whatever. In that case, one should object to preaching the gospel under any circumstances to any people and should see no utility at all in becoming acquainted with the Bible.[5]

Baptists came through confusion generated by false Calvinism with a more vibrant theology of means without sacrificing their unalloyed proclamation of the freedom of God in salvation. A use of ordained means for conversion is the responsibility of the evangelist; but just as clearly he is responsible for a full display of the truth that casts the sinner without strength before the mercy of God.

The Example of Samuel Pearce

The beloved friend of Fuller, Samuel Pearce (1766–1799), personified the living relation between doctrinal purity and passion for God's glory in evangelism.[6] Pearce participated with boundless energy and sacrifice in the Particular Baptist Missionary Society work and served as editor of the *Periodical Accounts*. Cathcart's *Encyclopedia* calls him "one of the warmest advocates of foreign missions that dwelt on earth since the Son of Mary came from his heavenly home on a foreign mission to this lost world." He has been compared to Robert Murray McCheyne and David Brainerd for combination of fervent piety and zeal. Not only did he promote the mission cause in England with all his might, but he also urged William Rogers of the Philadelphia Association to begin a

Baptist foreign mission society in America that would involve the energies of the entire denomination.

Since Americans, in Pearce's observation, so readily formed societies to support "arts, liberty, and emigration," and he wondered if there were not a few "found among them who would form a society for the transmission of the word of life to the benighted heathen."[7]

Pearce also nurtured a deep desire to go to the heathen himself and studied the Bengalee language in preparation for that purpose. He prayed unremittingly, examined his desires and motives with uncanny balance, and considered the radical imbalance between the availability of gospel preaching and the concentration of paganism rationally compelling. When he began to learn that the Missionary Society felt hesitant about sending him, he reflected, "I do think, however, if they knew how earnestly I pant for the work, it would be impossible for them to withhold their ready acquiescence."[8] Pearce's zeal for God's glory, surpassingly brilliant but analogous to the same desire in many of his friends and close associates, found nurture in an association that consistently defined itself in terms of a succinct doctrinal abstract:

> Maintaining the important Doctrine of Three Equal Persons in the Godhead,—Eternal and Personal Election,—Original Sin,—Particular Redemption,—Free Justification by the righteousness of Christ imputed,—Efficacious Grace in Regeneration,—the Final Perseverance of the Saints,—the Resurrection of the Dead,—The General Judgment at the Last Day,—the Life Everlasting,—and the Independence of their respective Churches:[9]

In a circular letter that Pearce wrote in 1794, he pointed particularly to the truth that God uses ordained means to accomplish his sovereign decreed will.[10] "There is not one doctrine in the gospel but what is 'according to godliness,'" Pearce wrote, and quickly added, "nor one promise of future happiness unconnected with present holiness." In the same way, if the Bible teaches us "the doctrine of God's everlasting love and his sovereign choice of his people," it also teaches us that they "are predestinated to be conformed to the image of Christ . . . through sanctification of the Spirit, and belief of the truth." Our Redeemer's "efficacious sacrifice" certainly removes the iniquity of his people and just as certainly purifies "unto himself a peculiar people, zealous of good works" (Titus 2:14 KJV).

Given the certainty of the decree as executed through the means, Pearce implored his hearers that they "let not shame, or the fear of displeasing men, withhold you from an attempt to lead sinners to Christ." They are not ashamed of their master, why should Christians be ashamed of theirs? You know little? But you know Christ and him crucified. You have little time? Fill it then all the more with service to God. What will you regret in a dying hour? Your lack of expending yourself for eternal purposes. "Finally," Pearce rose to a crescendo, "think what pleasure it will give you at the judgment day to meet and spend eternity with some to whose salvation you have been instrumental; such a circumstance would add fresh energy to your joy, and lustre to your crown."

Pearce's whole life, according to Fuller, was in itself a work of evangelism. In summing up distinguishing traits of his character, Fuller remarked, "It was love that expanded his heart, and prompted him to labour in season and out of season for the salvation of sinners."[11] In his visits to the sick, in his counsels, cautions, and reproofs, in his faithful censures, in his preaching of the gospel, holy love motivated him with the hope that Christ would be honored through the salvation of sinners. The news of conversion generated in him an indescribable joy. He wrote a friend after hearing that three daughters had been converted.

> Thanks, thanks be to God for the enrapturing prospects before you as a *father*, as a *Christian father* especially. What, *three* of a family! And these three at once! Oh the heights and depths, and lengths and breadths of his unfathomable grace! My soul feels joy unspeakable at the blessed news. Three immortal souls secured for eternal life! Three rational spirits preparing to grace Immanuel's triumphs, and sing his praise! Three examples of virtue and goodness, exhibiting the genuine influence of the true religion of Jesus before the world!—Perhaps three mothers training up to lead three future families in the way to heaven. Oh what a train of blessings do I see in this event! Most sincerely do I participate with my dear friend in his pleasures, and in his gratitude.[12]

Pearce's zeal and passion for souls expressed itself in careful, deliberate, determined, multifaceted evangelistic work. Preaching, personal interviews, letters of a deeply engaging and cross-centered affection combined in his efforts to be used to draw sinners to embrace Christ as Savior. He took great pains in his ardent and perspicuous presentation of Christ as the only hope of sinners and equally as great pains to ascertain that any apparent movement to Christ involved no manipulation on his part. He presented the truth with joy and certainty and relied on its compelling nature and the effectual drawing of God's Spirit for evangelistic success.

A letter written to a bewildered and speculative young man gives us a model of Pearce's understanding of the work of evangelism. This letter followed a conversation Pearce had engaged in with this person while traveling. A congenial endorsement of the benefits of cautious skepticism in matters of great importance initiated Pearce's approach to his young friend. "While examining the grounds of persuasion, it is right for the mind to hesitate," for every objection should be allowed to have its weight. "The more numerous and forcible objections are, the more cause shall we finally have for the triumph *'Magna est veritas et prevalebit.'*"

Several positive ideas must be weighed carefully, Pearce recommended, for they are weighty indeed. The importance of truth in general, but more particularly the leading item of the New Testament, Jesus Christ and him crucified, must be given preeminence. This central idea was no small claim: "The Creator of all things, out of mere love to rebellious men, exchanged a throne for a cross, and thereby reconciled a ruined world to God." None can deny that this is the burden of the apostolic message.

If that truth claim is deemed untenable, one must jettison the entire New Testament and then along with it the Old Testament. How can this be done, however, in light of "all the powers of evidence on which, as on adamantine pillars, its authority abides"? In pushing aside the Bible, "the infidel has more to reject than the believer to embrace." One receives it as authoritative, not from ancestral tradition, but "on the invincible conviction which attends an impartial investigation of its evidences."

Pearce gave a quick but arresting display of evidences for biblical authority and an overview of the beauty of the Bible's doctrines, particularly that which combines "the equitable and merciful perfections of the Deity in the sinner's salvation." This salvation does not create carelessness in the sinner but inspires him with "the liveliest hope" and makes him habitually devoted "to the interest of morality and piety." Pearce then exclaimed, "Such a doctrine I cannot but venerate; and to the *author* of such a doctrine my whole soul labours to exhaust itself in praise."[13]

Second to the importance of truth, Pearce reminded his skeptic, "man is a depraved creature." He painted a dark picture of the practical effects of depravity—

"so depraved that his judgment is as dark as his appetites are sensual, wholly dependent on God, therefore, for religious light as well as true devotion, yet such a dupe to pride as to reject every thing which the narrow limits of his comprehension cannot embrace, and such a slave to his passions as to admit no law but self-interest for his government." In light of that reality, he must realize that the human mind tends not to give due credence to evidences for a doctrine that is holy and assaults its pride. To err to the side of sinful dispositions is indeed human. We should learn, therefore, to distrust negative judgment when it opposes truths "too sublime for our understandings, or too pure for our lusts" and concede the truth of the gospel of Christ.[14]

If it indeed be true, then, third, it must heartily be embraced. Honey pleases through its taste, and the sun warms when we are exposed to its rays. So the heart is satisfied when it is given to God. Speculations will never seal the case. We must be Christians or infidels. "My son," saith God, "give me thine heart" (Prov. 23:26 KJV).

Pearce concluded his letter with a warm encouragement and confidence that his young friend would find salvation in Christ. "A humble admission of the light we already have is the most effectual way to a full conviction of the truth of the doctrine of Christ." In thus closing with Christ, he would "become assured that there is salvation in no other name than that of Jesus Christ: and thus from an inward experience of the quickening influences of his Holy Spirit" and would join the chorus of those singing the praises of Christ. "Yes, I yet hope—I expect—to see you rejoicing in Christ Jesus" as a living witness that he who earnestly seeks will find.

Pearce pointed his inquirer directly to Christ but in doing so assumed a prior agreement with the doctrine of the cross, the inspiration of Scripture, the depravity and deceitfulness of the human heart, and the willingness of Christ to save all who come to him on gospel terms. Pearce's evangelism involved ongoing instruction in biblical truth but always kept before the eyes Christ himself in whom all the riches of salvation and eternal glory reside. God must instruct, enlighten, and change the heart, but the evangelist must always move straight to the necessity of Christ and the immediate responsibility of such depraved sinners to trust him.

The Pastoral Evangelism of Andrew Fuller

Fuller's instruction to church members on personal evangelism follows the same pattern as modeled by Pearce in his brief evangelistic letter.[15] Fuller called for church members to qualify themselves for this task. First, they must be affectionate toward such seekers and be able to recommend the way of salvation with freeness and with joy. They must feel the importance of these matters, speak often of them, and be convinced that the Lord will do sinners good.

Next they must be "skilful in the word of righteousness." This involves the right execution of two important tasks, one negative and the other positive. First, we must not assume that every person who expresses interest either understands the gospel or is willing to be saved by it. Fuller dealt with a particular error associated with hyper-Calvinism, expressed by John Brine above, whereby some people sought internal evidence that they already had "an *interest* in Christ and spiritual blessings." Such persons desire private assurance that Christ purchased for them and was determined to give to them in particular the blessings of salvation. These understand neither the operations of grace nor their own sinfulness and the deceitfulness of their hearts. They operate from a subtle sense of self-righteousness and refuse to come to Christ in a gospel way, that is, that God is "willing to save any sinner that is willing to be saved" by Christ as set forth in the gospel.[16] If a person is not saved, it is because he stumbles at the stumbling stone.

Positively, the soul winner must point sinners "directly to the Saviour." Fuller took the view of New England theologian Samuel Hopkins, that sinners must be pointed immediately to Christ, not to the use of means. The evangelist must not give the sinner any place to stop and rest before he gets to Christ. He must advocate no means, no waiting at the pool, no use of ordinances, but only repentance from sin and trust in Christ. He must not be led to believe that "duties performed while in unbelief are pleasing to God."[17] In distress of mind, no consolation may be given apart from going to Christ. "What must I do to be saved?" demands the answer, "Believe on the Lord Jesus Christ."

Evidence of a person's being in Christ demands quite a different answer and a more introspective and investigative approach, but the only safe approach for the non-Christian is insistence on immediate closure with Christ. The duty of immediate repentance does not make doctrinal exposition less important. An evangelistic pastor and soul winner must "labour to make the sinner sensible of his sin, (as till this is the case he will never come to the Saviour)." A warrant to believe and come immediately to Christ is intrinsic in the gospel itself, not in any internal title or qualification to believe. More often than not, however, response is not immediate but calls for a careful destruction of false refuges and instruction of the understanding. Again, Fuller felt this tension and placed the duty of immediate response in the proper context. "The gospel itself is the warrant, and not any thing in the state of the mind; though, till the mind is made sensible of the evil of sin, it will never comply with the gospel."[18]

Caught between the extreme subjectivity of hyper-Calvinist views of the warrant to believe and the superficial Sandemanian views of mere assent to biblical fact, Fuller waged a war for true evangelism on two fronts. Overreaction to hyper-Calvinism tended to make evangelism less concerned about theology in general and the nature of conviction of sin and evidences of regeneration in particular. What for Fuller was a carefully articulated and doctrinally integrated understanding of God's sovereignty, human responsibility, and the bondage resulting from human depravity moved, particularly in the American context, toward a decisionistic, almost Sandemanian,[19] view of faith.

Chapter 5

Baptists Must Recover the Work of Evangelism, Part II

A Delicate and Delightful Equipoise

In the nineteenth century a growing number of evangelicals introduced substantial theological changes that redefined the practice of evangelism both in content and in method. A challenge confronted all Christians who believed in the necessity of conversion and the desirability of revival. Among Baptists in America, the Fuller/Pearce paradigm predominated through the first half of the century, even through the conflict with the antimission society movement. They were not as successful, however, in standing firm against a storm of a different type. Only gradually did this beautiful combination of truth and practice succumb to the falsely attractive and disfiguring forces of pragmatism.

W. F. Broaddus represents a group of Baptist ministers committed to evangelism and missions in a historically confessional framework. He led in the formation of the Salem Union Association in Virginia for the purpose of uniting several missionary churches. The association produced a document entitled *Sketch of Our*

Views of Divine Truth. In the first six articles, the association affirmed human depravity, the obligation to preach the gospel to every creature, the necessity of the Spirit's work, the sinner's recognition that salvation is all of grace and dependent on the blood and righteousness of Christ, the certain perseverance of those so called and justified, and the harmony between God's predestination and the instrumentality of means. Article 7 showed the irony of the errors of "antinomians" and "Arminians."

> We believe that it is the duty of all who hear the Gospel to believe and obey it. This we gather from the fact that our Lord himself and his Apostles commanded it in their addresses to men. We have often been struck with the likeness on this subject, between Antinomians and Arminians. It is true their systems are hostile to each other; but they alike contend that obligation to obey grows of grace conferred. The Antinomian says "God would not require men to do what they have not moral capacity to do: therefore it is not man's duty to believe in Christ, until he is divinely illuminated." The Arminian says "God would not require men to do what they have no moral capacity to do: therefore all men have power to believe in Christ, because all men are required to believe in him." We dissent from both. We believe that no man *will* come to Christ until he is divinely illuminated; and yet that every man is bound to do so, and accountable for not doing so, because his inability, consisting solely in the alienated state of his affections, is itself a *crime* and cannot therefore be an excuse for his unbelief. It does seem to us that those brethren who deny that it is the duty of all men to believe in Christ, while they charge us with Arminianism, are themselves much more justly liable to the charge, and are at the same time, furnishing the guilty with an excuse for their unbelief.[1]

This healthy integration of the sinner's absolute dependence on sovereign mercy and his immediate and absolute responsibility to repent of sin and find in Christ his full sufficiency for salvation produced both zeal and God-centeredness in Baptist evangelism.

The Pragmatizing of a Biblical Practice: The Challenge Begins

In spite of such a chastened approach to the use of means, the symbiotic relation between theology and means gradually declined as *means* ate up theology. The protracted meeting and the traveling evangelist, popularized through the camp meetings of the Second Great Awakening (ca. 1800) and the subsequent systematization of revival (ca. 1830), gradually squirmed into Baptist life. Controversy, resistance, and reserved toleration preceded the encroachment of these new evangelistic practices; they were not adopted without warning and sometimes lamentation.

David Benedict (1779–1874), a nineteenth-century pastor and Baptist historian in America, witnessed many of the unusual events of the Second Great Awakening at the turn of the century in the churches of the East and in the frontier camp meetings. The Methodists quickly adopted as a method that which had been an occasion for the mighty convicting and converting power of God. Benedict observed that something false and affected infused the regularizing of the method. Since they observed "many evident and remarkable displays of divine power" in these meetings, they evidently "considered them the most probable means of effecting a revival." For this reason, they "are industriously kept up by the Methodists throughout the United States."

> It is well known that they take much pains, by giving lengthy notice of their approach, by advertising them in newspapers, &c. to collect as large an assemblage of people as possible, and then, by preconcerted and artful manoeuvres, and by a mechanical play upon the passions, to produce that animation and zeal, which, at the times above-mentioned, were spontaneous and unaffected.[2]

William Fristoe (1742–1828), pastor and historian of the Ketocton Baptist Association in Virginia, saw the Methodist influence as a threat to biblical evangelism. Many under "considerable awakenings" found their way to these "strange physicians of souls" who would ensnare the "unguarded and ignorant" in order "to increase their number." According to Fristoe, these ministers worked diligently in opposition to the doctrine and implications of human depravity and moral helplessness, the necessity of sovereign, efficacious, unfrustrable grace, the necessity of imputed righteousness, and the certain efficacy of Christ's atoning work. Instead, they pointed to the "unering [sic] rule laid down by our progenitor [John Wesley], and adopted by our people, that makes it quite easy for every member of the community." Fristoe then depicted a scene of affectation of passion and bodily agitation that he observed in Methodist camp meetings that made the seeker insensible. As soon as the ability to reflect returned, he was declared converted.[3]

Baptists in the South, following the Methodist lead, began to use the same methods. Fristoe had observed the beginnings of this. He described the manner of this innovation.

> In some few instances among us, in addition to preaching the gospel in its simplicity, something of human invention, or contrivance, have been brought forward to aid the good work, such as these—when done preaching, the preacher passing thro' the congregation singing an hymn on some tender and affecting subject, with a tune of mournful sound, or if thought proper, of lively cheerful sound; for when this method is adopted there is not a certain rule to go by, and the people are to be taken as they are found. The above is accompanied with shaking of hands and exhortations with a great appearance of affection; by these means soft and tender passions have been wonderfully wrought upon, and some have expressed their desire to be prayed for, and sometimes enquiry is made whether some do not desire to be prayed for; the person or persons affected fall on their knees, at the preacher's feet, while prayer is made for them—all this is done with an air of solemnity, as much as possible, that it may affect all around; why such a mode of conduct has been adopted by any, is not so easy to say; to suppose, for a moment that it has been done to ingratiate themselves into the esteem of the people, and so make their way easier though the world seems too severe and harsh, or that they thought they could effect and bring about the conversion of souls by human exertion, cannot be admitted. We are ready to conclude that as anti-christ has been so successful in making proselytes by this means, that the honest and sincere have been ensnared; and led away by a misguided zeal, and lost sight of the unerring word of truth, and the primitive example of the faithful.[4]

This description of an early nineteenth-century phenomenon among Baptists calls for several observations. (1) Fristoe clearly viewed this as an unwarranted, unscriptural innovation, a "contrivance." (2) These occasions were recent and rare. (3) They were conducted in a solemn way. (4) He did not consider the actions motivated either by covetousness or a creature-centered orientation toward conversion. (5) Misguided zeal had moved sincere men who believed in the inerrancy of Scripture to ignore its implications in their evangelism by introducing these actions for which the Bible gave no instruction.

W. T. Brantly (1787–1845) looms large in Baptist life from 1811 until his death in Charleston, South Carolina, in March 1845. He served as pastor of several churches, including First Baptist Church of Philadelphia, Pennsylvania. While there the revival movement of the 1830s attracted his attention and his participation. Brantly examined the new methods with his usual thoroughness and insight. He found much about which to be cautious but also much to commend. His love of action in the Christian life prompted him to commend the use of protracted meeting and the anxious seat. When employed under the guidance of the doctrine of sovereign grace, he thought they were legitimate means for God's conversion of sinners. Brantly felt that many Baptists were too squeamish about these matters.

As Basil Manly Sr. (1798–1868) saw the development of the call for physical movement in the camp meetings, he felt dejected. Perhaps Brantly would have thought him squeamish, but Manly believed the measure introduced false criteria for gospel faithfulness. Such physical movement constituted the "criterion of good effects these days," but he was determined that he would never fall in with them. Preachers with less than half the talent and not one whit of the doctrinal content of Manly were able to "raise a perfect storm of passions, and lay them down in heaps around them apparently convicted of sin." Manly stated frankly and fervently his dislike for such a method and his stout refusal to adopt it.[5]

The Challenge Gains Momentum

The Religious Herald, a Baptist newspaper in Virginia, carried three articles by George Boardman Taylor (1832–1907) in 1861 on the subject of "Protracted Meetings." Taylor, the son of J. B. Taylor, later served for thirty-four years (1873–1907) as a Southern Baptist missionary to Italy. He recognized that controversy existed over the use of this measure, particularly with the anxious seat and the inquiry meetings used as an organic extension of the meetings. Taylor preferred the inquiry meetings over the anxious seat though he was "far from opposing anxious seats, as they are called." The most preferable inquiry meeting, in Taylor's opinion, occurred in the home of the sinner who had indicated a disturbed conscience. He also approved of the use of outside evangelists and reasoned along scriptural lines in its defense.

Some dangers, however, should be observed carefully and avoided with meticulous care. He insisted that *truth* should dominate "as distinguished from mere appeals to the feelings." The *doctrines* of "total depravity, helplessness, the certainty and justice of eternal punishment, as well as the free offers of the Gospel" must be prominent. "Mere physical excitement should be discouraged" and "solemn stillness" is much preferred over "impassioned appeals." "Overmuch effort, whether private or public, to induce persons to . . . profess their hope" should be avoided. The insistent reiteration of the truth will bring those who are "duly affected" to make the "proper manifestation."

Meanwhile, great care must be taken in dealing with those who indicated that they indeed were "inquirers." It was scarcely enough to tell an inquirer to believe, but the minister "must probe his heart, by getting him to speak freely of himself and of his exercises, and this cannot well be done in the brief time after the sermon." Great care should be taken in leading persons "to profess conversion" by rising or giving some other sign during a song. They are very apt to "mistake sympathy and excitement for conversion." The truly converted generally can be ascertained "in some more private way not open to the danger named."

Not only should caution characterize our dealings with the inquirer, but the purity of the church must be considered. Taylor felt revulsion at "this rushing into the church utter strangers, who come forward for prayer, profess conversion and propose to join," all on the same occasion. No one should partake of the membership in the church or its ordinances "ignorantly or rashly."[6]

Again in 1866 the issue of "protracted meetings" hit the newsstand in the *Religious Herald*.[7] The writer this time was the editor, J. B. Jeter, a prominent voice for orthodoxy among Baptists in the South, beloved pastor, and noted author. He provided five articles on the subject. Jeter believed that protracted meetings had scriptural foundations and that, abuses acknowledged, the benefits of these meetings "have greatly overbalanced their evils." After the fashion of Jonathan Edwards, he described many of the evils as endemic to the imbalance of human nature under the powerful influences of genuine religious impressions. These could not be avoided entirely, but they could be largely overcome if the "word is preached with discrimination," excesses firmly restrained, inquirers "carefully instructed, and discouraged from making a hasty and inconsiderate profession of faith."

Jeter encouraged churches to make energetic preparations for these meetings through prayer and special preaching designed to secure self-examination and interest in the salvation of sinners. Several means should be used to promote the meeting. In preaching "the understanding must be convinced by lucid arguments, the conscience aroused by stinging appeals, the affections stirred by pathetic addresses, and the soul won by the attractions of the cross." Also useful were reading Scripture, prayer, singing, and religious conversation. "Bad singing is a great hindrance in many protracted meetings" according to Jeter. Religious conversation could prove helpful because "it is the reproach of Christianity that it has been almost entirely banished from the social circle."

Beyond these ordinary means which have clear biblical warrant, Jeter argued for the use of the anxious seat and inquiry meetings as not only "authorized but indirectly required." Anecdotal evidence dominated his presentation. When the souls of sinners were at stake, "all means for its attainment seemed to be reasonable, desirable and authorized." In a strange twist of analysis, Jeter canonized the use of the anxious seat as a necessary demonstration of true repentance. While professing its neutrality, the resistance that it promoted in some sinners made the use of it necessary in their particular case. A humanly contrived stumbling block became a divinely ordained test of repentance in Jeter's discussion. He noted the following in the case of one person resolved not to go the way of the anxious seat.

> He had gradually approached nearer to the anxious seats, and just before the close of the service, he rushed forward, and with an outburst of intense feeling, prostrated himself at one. The struggle was over. His prejudice was slain, his pride was laid in the dust, the fear of men was banished, and, in short, the man was converted. There was no necessity that he should go to the anxious seat, except that he had resolved that he would not go, even to secure his salvation, and with that feeling, his conversion was impossible. That purpose renounced, the stronghold of Satan was demolished, and the man was a joyful captive of conquering grace.

He followed this anecdote with further discussion and illustrations earnestly urging his readers to see the great advantages of this measure. "When that step is taken by an enlightened, earnest well balanced mind, the way of retreat is closed, and nothing remains but to press forward to the cross and to victory." The anxious bench tended to break down perverseness of will, pride, a scornful attitude, fear of men, and the spirit of procrastination. A refusal to comply with the measure revealed to some degree the state of the heart. In summary:

> Going forward to an anxious seat, though it may deepen religious impressions and strengthen good resolutions, and by these means tend to secure a man's conversion, is, by no means, a condition of salvation. Yet we have rarely known persons to be converted in meetings, in which anxious seats were used, that refused to occupy them. In general, the same pride, worldliness, prejudice, indecision and scepticism which prevent them from occupying these seats, or making a public manifestation of their religious concern, keep them away from Christ.

Though Jeter recognized that the anxious seat had no straightforward biblical sanction, his endorsement of its practical usefulness established it as a true indicator of repentance. Not only did he push aside the regulative principle of biblical authority; he unwittingly embraced both a stumbling block and a false point of assurance. Willingness to go to the anxious bench gave evidence of repentance, and shyness about that particular physical movement or place showed that the heart still resisted Christ.

One could just as easily justify the Roman Catholic confessional on the basis of such reasoning. The conclusion that there is equal spiritual benefit intrinsic to both is not unreasonable.

Resistance Strong, but Losing Ground

More than twenty years later, however, the artifice of the anxious seat halfway house had still not become universal. Its effectuality in producing visible results had been adopted by a growing number of evangelists, but the churches and pastors were ambivalent over the true spirituality of the converts. Cathcart's *Baptist Encyclopedia* made a curious notation in its discussion of Jacob Knapp (1799–1874), a Baptist evangelist for forty-two years. The author wrote, "His preaching was doctrinal, direct, unsparing, even sometimes to the verge of coarseness; but his power over audiences was remarkable, and the fruits of his long toil in his chosen sphere, while not always genuine, were believed in many cases to be so, and always abundant." The description should be deposited in a museum of sentences as a model of studied reservation and faint praise.

That description summarizes the hesitations many Baptists still had about the methods gradually enveloping the churches. The anxious seat gave way to the invitation formula. Evangelists began to call people to come immediately to the front of the congregation and stand with the preacher as an indication of their intention to be saved. Both the deportment of the evangelist and the approvedness of his fruit puzzled, bewildered, frustrated, and sometimes alarmed thoughtful ministers.

W. E. Hatcher (1834–1912) had opportunity to observe evangelists and their methods as well as the responses of churches to them. Hatcher served faithfully and brilliantly in churches and gained a reputation as a "successful preacher in pro-tracted meetings, . . .a man of rare and varied gifts, . . . a remarkable sermonizer, . . . an earnest and most effective proclaimer of the soul-saving truths of the gospel" (Cathcart). He expressed this mixed verdict in the opening paragraph of an article entitled "The Modern Evangelist."

> Sometimes he has been welcomed with swelling enthusiasm, attended by mellow and responsive throngs, praised in terms superlative, feasted on milk and honey, loaded with costly gifts, and profusely wept over when he departed. At other times the tide has gone against him. Critics have plucked his famous sermons into tatters, denounced his methods as the wiles of a trickster, cast contempt on his processes of Christian consecra-tion, laughed to scorn his arithmetical array of conversions, and stigma-tized his platform manners as boorish and unbearable.[8]

Hatcher stated clearly that he had "chiefly in mind the Baptist evangelist." He was not opposed to the office or to the usefulness of protracted meetings. Several artifices, however, threatened to undo any good that might be gained from them. Though he preached the gospel, "he presents it in a dangerously mechanical way" like a "street peddler" with a "new nostrum for toothache." Sinners may march up to get it. If they don't take the remedy, he insisted on "some partial advance on their part, such as bowing or standing, or holding up their hand, or some other manifestation."

The evangelist massaged these methods to evoke or produce response where no "religious feeling" existed. "The prolonged and persistent attempts often made to precipitate professions of faith are simply infamous." His reputation hung on his suc-cess, crowds were valued for their overflow, converts were counted by the hand-shake, great and immediate results must be manifest every night. So hung his reputation on this apparent greatness that he was tempted to "excessive manipulation" and he hid "his failures under the guise of fictitious successes."

Hatcher saw churches adopting this style of immediate decisionistic evangelism "with results to be deplored." But the "revival machinery" now "stands in the way of the work it was designed to advance." That "work" that was impeded by such methods was the work of evangelism. Hatcher's timely and insightful protest, his call for those who "trust in the Holy Spirit and not in methods for producing conversion," his warning against those who are "clamorous for instantaneous results" could well be transferred to the twenty-first century.

A Contemporary Crisis

The concept of invitation no longer means what Andrew Fuller meant by it when he spoke of invitations as directly adapted as means to bring the lost to Christ. He called for preachers to press on the conscience every truth of divine revelation in its theological richness. The entire sermon should argue with such urgency that sinners would know that they must come to Christ and that they are welcome to come to Christ. Every message must subserve the point of Bunyan's great sermon, "Come and Welcome to Jesus Christ." The sinner comes not to the front at the end of a service but from sin and to Christ with his mind, his heart, his soul. The task is to lay siege to the soul with a bombardment of truth set on fire by love.

Another truth, however, is equally urgent for the sake of souls, the purity of the church, and the church's witness to the truth and character of God. That truth consists of a knowledge of the travail of the soul under the labor pains of the new birth. The Spirit's operation is mysterious and thorough and seldom follows any man-made script. While immediacy is pressed as the sinner's duty, painstaking patience and submission to the just prerogative of merciful convictions of God must not be shoved aside.

We have become very proficient as well as persistent in evangelistic immediacy. Techniques and exhortations about the public invitation appear frequently, both in books and in conference sermons. Uniformly, they advocate a physical action on the part of the person seeking salvation and assure him that such action is the same as biblical repentance and faith. One writer told inquirers, even if they did not know what they needed, "Don't worry about what to say when you get here. By your coming as an inquirer you will be saying, 'I want to go God's way today and trust in Him.' And when you come, 'Your sins He'll wash away.'" This action culminated in a recommended five- to fifteen-minute counseling session. That closed with a salvation prayer outlined point by point by the worker. One who recommended a book on invitation techniques called them "tested and proved techniques simple to understand, easy to follow and guaranteed to produce results."

This type of evangelism is set forth confidently as the answer to church stagnation among Southern Baptists. Zeal to get more baptisms will heal us, so we have taught and exhorted for decades.

Zeal without knowledge, however, kills. Proficiency in provoking decisions has replaced pastoral care and wisdom. Sometimes telling a person how to make a decision may not be evangelism at all. On occasions, encouraging a sinner to continue in pursuit of the grace of God would be more biblical and apostolic (Acts 13:42–43, 48). In Acts 28, Paul engaged the Jews "from morning until evening" (v. 23) in a detailed biblical and theological discussion on the nature of the kingdom of God and the credentials of Jesus of Nazareth to meet the Old Testament qualifications for being Messiah. Some believed and some did not, but none could say they had not been dealt with thoroughly and respectfully. Perhaps less baptisms with greater pastoral and church discernment would be better than more baptisms under the same programmatic conditions that have governed the last fifty to seventy-five years.

The *prima facie* impression of some vital statistics suggests this conclusion. Since the Sunday school attendance campaign entitled "A Million More in '54," Southern Baptists have baptized 19,677,550 people. Total membership as of 2003 stood at 16,315,050. For the same year, resident membership—those who live within the church field of their membership—was 11,248,022. Sunday school enrollment for that year was 8,193,886 and average attendance in Sunday school was 4,119,732. Of course, enrollment and attendance includes many children and young people in families that are not yet church members. Average attendance in morning worship for 2003 was 5,873,880, noting the same caveat of visitors, young people, and children not church members. Only between 25 percent and 35 percent of current membership gives any regular attention to Bible study and worship within the corporate community of the church.

A 2003 survey by the Rainer Group given to carefully selected churches in a "client group" involved 1,577 members of those churches. The survey indicated that 22 percent of Southern Baptists do not believe in the exclusivity of Christ for salvation. How did someone who does not believe in the exclusivity of Christ become a member of a Baptist church? How does the person who holds that position think he is a Christian? He certainly cannot have the conviction that Ann Judson had at the time of her conversion (1806).

> I felt myself to be a poor lost sinner, destitute of everything to recom-
> mend myself to the divine favor: That I was, by nature, inclined to
> every evil way; and that it had been the mere sovereign, restraining
> mercy of God, not my own goodness, which had kept me from com-
> mitting the most flagrant crimes. This view of myself humbled me in
> the dust, melted me into sorrow and contrition for my sins, induced
> me to lay my soul at the feet of Christ, and plead his merits alone, as
> the ground of my acceptance. I felt that if Christ had not died, to
> make an atonement for sin, I could not ask God to dishonor his holy
> government so far as to save so polluted a creature, and that should he
> even now condemn me to suffer eternal punishment, it would be so
> just that my mouth would be stopped, and all holy beings in the uni-
> verse would acquiesce in the sentence, and praise him as a just and
> righteous God.[9]

A person who experienced this kind of conversion, the only kind, could never see salvation as coming in any other way than through the atoning work of the incarnate Son of God.

Many nuances of meaning could be teased out of these basic statistics, but the implications are not encouraging. Devices for decision that simply raise the statistics of the number baptized will not help. Both church purity and theological integrity suffer under unreformed, uninformed zeal. Souls of sinners are deluded and the world is convinced that no difference is made by supposed Christian conversion. In 1880 Henry Tucker, the editor of the *Christian Index and Southwestern Baptist*, saw this trend developing and suggested the following solution.

> The remedy consists of two things: First, to exclude unworthy
> members. Second to be careful, hereafter, to admit none who are not
> worthy. Neither of these tasks is easy, but the first is Herculean. We
> have been so careless in the reception of members—so anxious to
> increase in numbers without regard to quality, that the moral tone of
> many of our churches is utterly debased, and there is not religious
> power enough to throw off the unworthy load. We are reaping the

harvest sown by the folly of our predecessors. We must be careful not to transmit such an inheritance to those who come after us. When the "success" of a pastor is estimated by the number excluded during his administration, rather than by the number baptized, a new and better era will have dawned. What we need is to *unload*.[10]

Some may find such a suggestion peculiar. They might think that not only is Tucker's idea counterintuitive but positively unevangelistic. In fact, his call is for a more sober look at evangelistic technique and a call for serious pastoral attention to this most important matter. His use of the word *unworthy* does not indicate a works righteousness as qualification for church membership; instead he called for preachers to know the marks of true repentance from sin and faith in the Lord Jesus. Churches must cease to be "careless" in this matter. Just adding numbers of baptisms while "moral tone" declines is pure folly and creates massive problems for future generations.

Churches must "unload" through serious Bible-centered church discipline in order to become a fit place for the birth of new spiritual children. Tucker argued that church holiness must serve as the foundation for meaningful evangelism.

A Correction with Far-Reaching Implications

The theological malaise which provided the womb for the gestation of the assault on biblical authority was itself the product of a shift in the relation of theology and evangelism. As evangelism became more "act-oriented" evangelism, the less it depended on theological persuasion. Maximizing the mechanistic predictability of methods produced a correlative minimizing of the importance of theology. When the success of evangelism is directly proportioned to theological reduction, then evangelistic zeal has little at stake in defending theological fullness.

The recovery of inerrancy, therefore, is only a first step and will not have its full effect until the work of evangelism has been recovered from its unstable decisionistic foundation. Recovering the basic biblical framework of law and gospel provides a good starting point for this.

Chapter 6

Baptists Must Recapture the Complementarity of Law and Gospel

The Bible Establishes the Issue

Tension over the issues of law and gospel have penetrated Christian history from the first century to the present. Jesus had conflict with the Jewish leaders and teachers over their misuse of the law. His heightened sense of the righteousness of the law and his submission to its curse in no sense diminished, but only enhanced, its place in the display of God's righteousness through the gospel. Paul's letter to the Galatians attacks the misuse of the law by the Judaizers. Their low view of its demands allowed them to prescribe its keeping as an element of our righteousness before God (Gal. 3:2, 10–13).

Paul had warned the Ephesians that false teachers would come in among them from their own number (Acts 20:30). His letter to Timothy indicates that this false teaching focused on a misuse of the law (1 Tim. 1:7). Paul reminded Timothy that the "law is good, if one uses it lawfully" (1 Tim. 1:8). Every erroneous teaching against which Paul warned Timothy to be on his guard can be seen as a failure to grasp the fundamental relationship between law and gospel.

The Witness of the Past

Within Puritanism and Baptist life, especially of the seventeenth, eighteenth, and early nineteenth centuries, the relationship of the law to the gospel fueled many controversies.[1] In 1786, the Particular Baptist Association of Warwickshire wrote its circular letter on the subject of antinomianism. Its second sentence stated, "Of all the errors with which the Christian church is, or ever has been, infested, none is in its nature more absurd, and in its consequences more subversive of all true religion, than the *libertine* doctrine of ANTINOMIANISM."[2]

Accusations of antinomianism filled the theological vocabulary of the eighteenth-century evangelicals. Sometimes those who appeared to be polar opposites skewered each other with the barbs of the same accusation, "Antinomian!" In reality, a measure of truth resides in these epithets hurled from opposing camps. Andrew Fuller gave some insight into this phenomenon.

> Let an attentive reader examine the system of Socinus, and even of Arminius, and he will find them agreed in opposing the native equity and goodness of the moral law. The former claims it as a matter of justice that allowances be made for human error and imperfection; and the latter, though it speaks of *grace,* and *mediation of Christ,* and considers the gospel as a new, mild, and remedial law, yet would accuse you of making the Almighty a tyrant, if this grace were withheld, and the terms of the moral law strictly adhered to. All these, as well as that species of false religion which has more generally gone by the name of *Antinomianism,* you see, are agreed in this particular. This last, which expressly disowns the moral law as a rule of life, sets up the gospel in opposition to it, and substitutes visionary enjoyments as the evidence of an interest in gospel blessings, in place of a conformity to its precepts.—This last, I say, though it professes to be greatly at variance with several of the foregoing schemes, is nearer akin to them than its advocates are willing to admit.[3]

Later Fuller described the confessional approach to the threefold use of the law with an emphasis on its evangelical use and its use as "the rule of life." He asserted that "we may safely consider it as a criterion by which any doctrine may be tried; if it be unfriendly to the moral law, it is not of God, but proceedeth from the father of lies."

Fuller was the heir of much clear thinking and skillful polemics on this issue. Benjamin Keach (1640–1704) in opposition to Richard Baxter focused on the law and justification. His sermons and treatises steadily insisted on a right understanding of law, gospel, righteousness, and holiness. Both the conviction of sin and understanding the necessity of the imputation of Christ's righteousness came from a submission to the purity, spirituality, and irrevocable standing of the moral law. Keach never retreated from preaching that "the righteousness, and Benefits of Christ's Righteousness, is made ours, when we relye, or trust to God's free promise as the immediate and sole Cause of Pardon and Life, (as all true Protestants formerly affirmed)."

One of the views that Keach opposed asserted that justification comes from a new covenant of diminished expectations so that our faith is accepted as obedience to the law and thus justifies. So taught Baxter. Not so, taught Keach: "If Christ fulfilled the Law for us, then (say I) that Obedience of his, must be imputed to us, as if we had wrought it, and so we, by the Application of the Righteousness, are justified in God's sight, from the Accusation of the Law, without any Works, or procuring Conditions, performed by us."[4]

John Gill (d. 1771), accused of antinomianism, does not seem to qualify as such. He heaped unmistakable disdain on all human works, all supposed works of the law, as containing any possible merit. Some moralists who thought the doctrine of imputed righteousness cut the moral nerve represented him as an opponent of the moral law. Related to justification, however, he clearly preached the law as the means by which a soul is brought into a state sensible of its sinfulness and condemnation. In addition, the law points to the righteousness and acceptability of the life and atoning work of Christ. Beyond that, though human good works even in the regenerate still are flawed and filled with sin, the law in the hand of Christ serves as a means of sanctification.

John Ryland Jr. (d. 1825), in *Serious Remarks on the Different Representation of Evangelical Doctrine,* engaged the dangers of antinomian doctrine. The antinomianism he opposed, while addressing the evangelical use of the law, concerned more pointedly the use of the law in progressive sanctification. Some had denied that such a spiritual reality as progressive sanctification existed and any use of the law for such a thing amounted to a denial of the gospel. Ryland responded:

> What can be designed by denying that the law is a rule of life to believers? Do these men suppose we mean it is a rule by which they are to *merit* life? Our Lord knows we are as far from this imagination as they can be; and as careful to prevent others from indulging it. But we are fully assured the most effectual and scriptural way of cutting up all *illegal* hopes by the root, is showing the strictness, extent, spirituality, and yet the excellence and equity of the divine law; even that law, which is summed up by the Apostle in one word, LOVE; which our Lord divides into two great commandments, requiring supreme love to God, and disinterested benevolence to man; which is farther ramified in the Ten Commandments; and fully explained in the whole preceptive part of the divine word.
>
> This was the law which the incarnate Son of God *delighted* to obey; it was in his *heart*, and he has promised to write it in the hearts of his people. Is it possible a genuine believer should despise it? What part of it is vacated by the interposition of our Redeemer? Which precept has he granted us a licence to violate? Has he lessened our obligations to love God; or our obligations to love our neighbour? Or can we show our love to God, by having more gods than one, by idolatry, by profaning his name, or by neglecting the Lord's-day? Can we manifest our love to man, without regarding those relative duties which are so expressly inculcated by Paul and Peter? Are we at liberty to kill, commit adultery, steal, bear false witness, or covet any thing that is our neighbour's. What duty is there required in the moral law, which the believer is not bound to perform? What sin is forbidden there, which he is at liberty to indulge?[5]

Richard Furman, preaching in Charleston in 1791, enunciated as a qualification for gospel ministry that one must have a clear understanding of how to "distinguish between the law and gospel." He must "point out the ruined and guilty state of all, by nature, under the curse of a broken law; sound, as it were, Mount Sinai's thunder in the sinner's ear." Sinners must know without equivocation that "by the deeds of the law, shall no flesh living be justified." Just as clearly, however, the preacher must point out Jesus as the "Lamb, who taketh away the sins of the world," one who is an almighty and willing Savior.[6]

C. D. Mallary (1801–1864) gained a large hearing among his contemporaries for his profound godliness. Mallary was a part of the committee that prepared the "Address to the Public" when the Southern Baptist Convention was formed. Cathcart's *Encyclopedia* describes him as a "man of most uncommon piety" who exerted "a more wholesome influence than any other man of the denomination in the State [Georgia]." He had "clear views of divine truth, and a deep experience of its sanctifying power in the heart." Because he was "thoroughly instructed in the Scriptures," he also was "profoundly conversant with the workings of experimental religion." Peppered throughout his edifying book *Soul Prosperity*, one finds the importance of accurate appraisals of law and gospel. One section defines the relationship between obligation and dependence. Here he gives this clear analysis.

> We are not to seek nor to expect justification by the deeds of the law; no, verily—that comes to us by the perfect righteousness of Christ. But shall we therefore encroach upon the strict claims of the law as our rule of life, as the guide and teacher of our inner man? Our want of conformity to its demands does not diminish its claims. Our *attainments* are one thing, our *duty* is another. The former are crowded with defects, and call for daily sorrow and for daily pardon; the latter calls for nothing less than a hearty and full compliance with all that God commands. A standard less elevated than this will leave us without chart or compass, throw every man upon his own dark, selfish, and capricious promptings, and by pulling down the views form [sic; *from*] the right mark, paralyze our efforts, reconcile us to dwarfish attainments, and at length fill the bosom with proud and swelling notions for having attained to a deceitful and imaginary perfection. What unscriptural reasonings sometimes creep into the bosoms of many that we would fain call the children of God! . . . Alas! Alas! These frames and feelings are often poor, rebellious, antinomian things! . . . Away with all this carnal heresy! God's eternal word is the standard. As the creatures of God are we bound to respect it in all things; as redeemed by the blood of Christ, our obligations are infinitely augmented to respect to all God's commands.[7]

Richard Fuller (1804–1876) reflects a consensus on this issue for the Southern Baptists of the nineteenth century in a sermon entitled "The Law and the Gospel." A picturesque and rhetorically powerful interweaving of the themes of law and gospel, the sermon presents a full exploration of both the evangelical and sanctifying uses of the law as it is seen in the context of the gospel. A succinct summary of these themes begins with the assertion that "the law has no efficacy to produce in us any conformity to the pattern it proposes." Rather, the gospel "possesses this wonderful property," that is, that it "charms away the power of corruption and transforms us to the righteousness of the law, at the very time that it absolves us from all the penalties of the law."

Fuller's sermon, built on Romans 8:3–4, pursued unrelentingly a display of the "wisdom and power of Jehovah" in devising a scheme of pure grace, "suprajudicial interference," by which lawbreakers find release from their punishment though each one would confess: "But mine are sins thou must not, canst not spare while heaven is true, and equity is thine." He then quoted from Romans 8:3–4.

> For what the law could not do, in that it was weak through the flesh, God sending his own Son in the likeness of sinful flesh, and for sin, condemned sin in the flesh: that the righteousness of the law might be fulfilled in us, who walk not after the flesh, but after the Spirit. (KJV)

Fuller's explanatory summary of his discussion crystallizes not only his sermon but the issue as it must be consciously addressed again as an element of Baptist witness.

> But, now—here is our second reflection—where the sacrifice of Calvary is truly accepted as the expedient by which, in the jurisprudence of heaven, the judicial righteousness of the law has been abundantly fulfilled *for us,* it will also, along with the sense of pardon, send its sanctifying power into our nature. By a mysterious influence which the world cannot comprehend, which can be known only by experience, it will win the heart to love and obedience, and will thus fulfill the moral righteousness of the law *in us.* "Do we make void the law through faith? God forbid; yea we establish the law." Not only does faith repair the outrage done to the majesty of the law by pleading the sublimest satisfaction, but it restores its dethroned supremacy over the heart and life.[8]

Fuller also reminded his generation, his church in Baltimore in particular, of the great personal comfort of the operations of grace to satisfy an outraged law. In November 1861, as his daughter lay dying, she had the keenest consciousness of acceptance before God because of the work of Christ specifically in relation to the law. As Fuller told her about how solicitous the church had been for her in prayer and how highly she was esteemed in their eyes, she responded, "Do not my dear father, I beg you, utter one word about me. Speak only of Jesus, his blood and righteousness. I am a poor sinner saved by grace, who feels her unworthiness, and laments that, having so short a life, she did not devote it more entirely to such a Saviour."

When asked how such assurance brightened the hours in which she faced death, she responded, "How? Did he not die for me? Does not his blood cleanse from all sin? . . . Washed in his blood, how can I doubt? Clothed in his spotless righteousness, what can I fear?" Fuller picked up this theme of his daughter's dying confidence as one of the elements of his sermon. "In the satisfaction of Calvary, God's justice is satisfied; for, on the very theatre which had witnessed the dishonor of the law, that law is vindicated and magnified: God's holiness is satisfied."[9]

The law therefore, in Fuller's view, must have a threefold fulfillment in the life of the believer. His sins, transgressions of the law, must be forgiven, his opposition to its holy character must be cured, and its demands for positive righteousness must be imputed. Fuller expressed this cogently in a sermon entitled "A Precious Saviour."

> To those who believe he is precious. They alone feel their guilt and corruption, the absolute necessity of a great atonement and the infusion of a holy nature by the Saviour. And they are conscious of something more. Even after pardon and the transfusion of a new principle of spiritual life, the Christian has to mourn over daily imperfections; and, at times, sin—though it cannot have dominion—breaks out with such alarming mutiny that he is kept low and abhors himself before God. He feels, therefore, the necessity of a righteousness not only imparted, but imputed;—a righteousness other than his own, if he is to stand perfect before inflexible Justice. Others are blinded, but he sees clearly that God must love us, or we are forever lost; that if God loves us, he must love our person, not our characters; and that, therefore, he must love us in Christ, clothed in his righteousness.[10]

The Message for Today

The struggles with law and gospel appear in the beginning of Baptist life and establish an agenda of vital questions. The necessity of contemporary attention to the issue arises from two concerns, one ecclesiological—or the maintenance of historic Baptist identity—and the second pastoral.

Moderate Baptists

As an issue of identity, antinomianism has made strange bedfellows with the moderate cause in Southern Baptist life. Though historically and doctrinally connected with hyper-Calvinism, the individualistic freedom from external guidelines propounded in antinomian views of assurance and sanctification have been attractive to at least one ardent defender of the moderate cause, Frank Louis Mauldin. The Particular Baptist preacher of the seventeenth century, Paul Hobson, espoused regeneration as an immediate indwelling of the Spirit resulting in a sinner's being "Christed." For Mauldin, this kind of immediacy gave just the right pretense for freedom. Christ's indwelling through his Spirit eliminated the validity of propositions and external guidelines. That false dichotomy between internal freedom and externally revealed authority summarizes the moderate assumptions about Baptist identity.

Mauldin summarizes Hobson's view of truth in its "Christological modes," for Christ is the "personal cause, object, and essence of truth." For this reason one may distinguish truth from falsehood "by means of an intimate acquaintance with Christ." Truth, according to Mauldin's view of Hobson, must not be equated with "comprehension, or with an intellectual assent to the truths of God"; just as surely eliminated is "a knowledge gained from properly understanding the law." No, none of the "speculative" ways of thinking will do for the apprehension of truth; rather it is a "supernatural light set up in the soule by God; the life of which light hath his residence in God." Mauldin then made this observation about Hobson's view as he made his pitch for historic Baptist views of truth.

> Hobson here pictures the relation of Christ and the Christian as that of an internal relationship, i.e., as a relation in which the terms related are affected or changed by the relation. In Christ, the believer is transformed into the very nature and glory of Christ. Hobson does not use figurative or metaphorical language in making this assertion. He

speaks descriptively. In the internal relation to Christ, the old self is "annihilated, and all turned into Christ; Hee is removed from his former center, his owne bottom; there is a new ingrafting and being carried up into Christ, so that he is transformed into the hidden, divine, superexcellent glory, and riches and life of Christ." The believer is in actuality made one with "the truth."[11]

That Mauldin interpreted Hobson entirely accurately may be called into question. Though his language startles with its imagery, many seventeenth-century Puritans discussed God's operations on the soul in similar manner. Hobson, perhaps, contra Mauldin, used language figuratively and metaphorically. His intent could easily be interpreted as the normal Puritan understanding of the immediacy of the work of the Spirit in regeneration and transformation of life. Suppose, however, that Mauldin was correct about Hobson. Hobson's view represents a fringe view of the Baptists that the majority disowned and fought against. If a person is "annihilated" and made one with "the truth," what need is there of law or Scripture? This kind of antinomianism was soon corrected by seventeenth-century Baptists. Ironically, it found no quarter in the Calvinist resurgence of the late twentieth century but came to rest among the moderate wing of Southern Baptists.

American Baptist Churches USA

Churches of the American Baptists have fallen prey to this annoying error. The 1970s–90s saw resolutions on human rights, freedom, Christian unity, and human sexuality. With the intent of affirming "the denominations' basic principles of freedom of thought and belief," these statements referred to John Bunyan, Roger Williams, and Martin Luther King as embodying historically the concerns the resolutions addressed. Even the greatly agitated controversy over sexuality called for a new attempt to "consider prayerfully the mind of Christ." The urgency given this issue arose from the acknowledgement that there "exists a variety of understandings throughout our denomination on issues of human sexuality such as homosexuality." Dialogue should proceed under the banner of commitments to "freedom," "the principle of liberty of conscience," "free inquiry and debate without restrictions or coercion," and "openness of mind and spirit."

Though the Bible provides source material and stands ostensibly as "central to our lives," a clear divide between a settled word and the "living Christ" determines the burden of the interpretative task. "The Christian faith is centered in a person," they argued. "It is not a legalistic code which forms our faith; it is the living Christ."

For "legalistic code" one should read "the historic consensus of Baptists on theological confession through the centuries." Baptists of former generations shared certain theological presuppositions no longer held by many Baptists in the modern ABC-USA. The defining authority of objective truth has no place in their concept of freedom, and it contradicts, in their opinion, the ongoing work of Christ in his people. Glenn Hinson, a Baptist aligned with the moderate cause among Southern Baptists, stated this principle when he said, "The name Baptist refers to that version of Christianity which places the priority of voluntary and uncoerced faith or response to the Word and Act of God over any supposed 'objective' Word and Act of God."[12] The fight to be free from an objective word indulges the spirit and basic principle of antinomianism.

Conservative Southern Baptists

More definitive inconsistencies on law and gospel still unsettle conservative Southern Baptists. Pastoral concerns over issues of justification, sanctification, assurance, and church discipline have direct connections with a healthy grasp of the conceptual relations between law and gospel. Some strategies of outreach and paradigms for church growth have pushed aside the law-gospel relationship for one that appears more immediately relevant. The minister's task, so it is assumed, is to present biblical principles as giving a sound foundation for day-to-day happiness and healthy relationships. Pressures of contemporary life, issues of personal insecurity and self-esteem, financial insolvency, perplexity in rearing children, marital unity, pleasing personal relationships and unresolved emotional conflict often dominate the sermonic menu of many evangelical and Baptist churches.

Though cloaked within an evangelical ethos and an ostensible commitment to biblical inerrancy and an undergirding motive of evangelism, the basic substance of biblical content, in such cases, goes little beyond the man-centered optimistic liberal message of the early twentieth century. Transcending the effectiveness of the liberal Harry Emerson Fosdick in this scheme of preaching and organization of church life would be extremely difficult. Fosdick presented a picture of the greatest diversity designed to fulfill everyone's perception of worship.

> Indeed, we have deliberately sought to make our services of worship inclusive of varied religious temperaments, so that under

Riverside's roof are housed week by week types of worship commonly housed under separate sectarian roofs. Each week we conduct one major congregational preaching service of the kind familiar in most nonliturgical Protestant churches; we conduct one liturgical service without sermon, composed mainly of music and litany; on every Sunday of the year we sponsor a Quaker service, run by the Friends themselves, some of whom are members with us; we conduct worship services where religious drama is central, and others where free discussion of religious problems is carried on. All these types meet real human needs and represent valid varieties of temperament, and we have put them under one roof.[13]

Did this grand scheme of broad appeal arise from a doctrinal commitment from Scripture? Fosdick says that in "implementing this idea we did not so much impose a prearranged program on the community as ask the community what it wanted from us." This diversity arose mainly, therefore, from the community's perceptions of its needs and desires. Some things, however, were prearranged: "bowling alleys, a gymnasium, a playground, theatrical stages."[14]

Even the major preaching service was held only because so many traditional Protestants felt more comfortable with the practice of that tradition. Fosdick did not see preaching as an ordinance of God mandated as central to every corporate worship experience. In fact, Fosdick did not "put preaching central in my ministry" but instead distrusted a "preacher to whom sermons seem the crux of his functioning." Fosdick, though celebrated as a preacher, saw the task as "personal counseling on a group scale." The task focused on dealing "directly with individual needs, . . . with personality's urgent needs, . . . dealing privately and intimately with the deep-seated problems of those whose servant he is supposed to be." The radio program, "National Vespers," he saw as a "means of vital dealing with the problems of real people."[15]

No serious evangelical would deny that a preacher must speak to the vital needs of his listeners. To define those needs, however, in terms of their own immediate perceptions, or in the categories of psychology, or in terms of present culture sidesteps the biblical analysis. The biblical message on law—that is, we all are under a verdict of condemnation and death—and gospel—that is, only one remedy will suffice for our deepest need, the Lord Jesus' atoning work and resurrection—constitutes the only message of the Christian pulpit. One who focuses on issues of the present age and gives help only for the present age does nothing more than Fosdick did—a man who did not even believe in the deity of Jesus, or his substitutionary atonement, or his bodily resurrection.

The approach of speaking immediately and fundamentally to felt needs betrays the biblical framework for confronting human ills. The understanding of condemnation and its remedy of atonement and imputed righteousness so prominent as a biblical theme flows immediately from the law-gospel construct. Even so is it true for the divine purpose of mortification of sin and increase of holiness. Law and gospel are at the center of that issue.

Assurance of salvation, including the ground for rational investigation of internal evidences of regeneration, and an individual's conformity of life to a biblical pattern of saving faith, comes only with serious consideration of the perpetuity of the law as an expression of the intrinsic holiness of God. Spiritual vitality and purity within the church suspend largely on these issues. It is in the context of law and gospel that doctrine and experience, both corporate and individual, radically and inextricably mesh.

Conclusion

A full and healthy recovery from the recent decades of doctrinal reductionism and corresponding heterodoxy awaits a renewed apprehension of the interconnections of the biblical themes of law and gospel. Misperceptions and misapplications of this issue within the pale of the conservative movement of Southern Baptists could eventually be more crippling to the recovery of biblical Christianity than the active opposition of the moderate movement.

Chapter 7

Recovery of a Grace-Centered Theology

Grace—a Biblical Idea

The relationship between law and gospel naturally brings up the issue of grace. Grace flows to sinners from the triune God and heightens the importance of holding a trinitarian understanding of salvation. Paul speaks of the "grace, which was given us in Christ Jesus before the world began" (2 Tim. 1:9 KJV). This is the same grace that Paul unfolds in Ephesians 1:3–14 in terms of the Father's election of persons before the foundation of the world and predestination of them to adoption. He reminds us that his beloved Son already stands as the covenantal guarantee of the certainty of these blessings. The Spirit's indwelling seals these blessings to the purchased possession—in both the whole as well as the members of it. In eternity the glory of this grace will be an object of praise.

> Blessed be the God and Father of our Lord Jesus Christ, who has blessed us with every spiritual blessing in the heavenly places in Christ, just as He chose us in Him before the foundation of the world, that we should be holy and blameless before Him. In love He predestined us to adoption as sons through Jesus Christ to Himself, according to the

kind intention of His will, to the praise of the glory of His grace, which He freely bestowed on us in the Beloved. [*All of these spiritual blessings promised by the Father and secured by the blood, burial, and bodily resurrection of the Son, and which now reside in Him to be obtained by union with him, and which form the substance of the preaching of the gospel certainly became yours when*] you were sealed in Him with the Holy Spirit of promise, who is given as a pledge of our inheritance, with a view to the redemption of God's own possession. (Eph. 1:3–14; words in italics are a paraphrase by author)

The full range of the gracious operations of the Trinity come to the fore again when Paul reminded Titus that we are "justified by His grace." (Titus 3:7)

> He saved us, not on the basis of deeds which we have done in righteousness, but according to His mercy, by the washing of regeneration and renewing by the Holy Spirit, whom He poured out upon us richly through Jesus Christ our Savior, so that being justified by His grace we would be made heirs according to the hope of eternal life. (Titus 3:5–7)

Also, to the Ephesians he wrote, "By grace are ye saved through faith; and that not of yourselves" (Eph. 2:8 KJV). Peter reminded the church at Jerusalem, "We believe that we are saved through the grace of the Lord Jesus, in the same way as they also are" (Acts 15:11). To encourage Timothy in ministry, Paul gave a concentrated look at the grace of the Lord Jesus Christ as peculiarly related to the salvation of hardened sinners. Christ sets men in the ministry to preach the gospel, for it is certain that those he came to save will hear it and repent. This explains the patience of Christ, gives warrant for confidence and perseverance in ministry, justifies prayer for all men all over the world, and justifies his own ministry to the Gentiles (1 Tim. 1:12–2:7). In all of this Paul can say that the "grace of our Lord was more than abundant" (1 Tim. 1:14).

Grace—a Christian Confession but Point of Division

With numerous other direct assertions of the grace-centeredness of salvation, no Christian group denies that sinners are saved by grace. The willingness of all historic Christian bodies to confess this has been made clear in ecumenical dialogues of recent years. On October 31, 1999, the 482nd anniversary of Martin Luther's posting of the 95 Theses, a number of Lutheran bodies signed a Joint Declaration with the Pontifical Council for the Unity of Christians. Years of discussion, writing, and rewriting preceded that historic event. One sentence, affirmed by both groups, shows that disagreements on salvation are not differences in which one group accepts grace and another group shuns grace. The sentence states: "By grace alone, in faith in Christ's saving work and not because of any merit on our part, we are accepted by God and receive the Holy Spirit, who renews our hearts while equipping and calling us to good works."[1]

Such mere ascription to grace hardly says it all, however, as should be plain for all to see. Controversy on this issue concerns the manner and locus of the operation of grace. Roman Catholicism locates grace within the sacraments to be distributed by the church. In addition, humans may contribute to their standing in justification by meritorious works done under the power of grace; that is, they assist their own justification by "freely assenting to and cooperating with" the "predisposing grace of God." This concept of grace as a cooperative venture is called *synergism.*

Also, baptism is called the instrumental cause of justification "without which no man was ever justified." In addition, justification consists of the sanctification and renewal of the inward man by the infusion of faith, hope, and love. This justification may be lost; in that event, penance, the second plank after shipwreck, provides grace for recovery of justification. All of this, of course, streams from the "merit of his [Christ's] passion."

Christ's work of satisfaction on the cross procures a body of grace in which sinners may participate by obedient submission to the church. "The meritorious cause is his most beloved only begotten Son, our Lord Jesus Christ, who, . . . merited for us justification by his most holy passion on the wood of the cross and made satisfaction for us to God the Father."[2] The Mass, through the perpetual sacrifice of Christ, provides the ongoing implementation of grace to the gradually justified sinner.

Protestantism, on the other hand, in general, locates grace not in the sacrament as an instrumental cause but in the direct action of God upon the mind and affections when a sinner hears the gospel. Faith comes by hearing. Such grace, in a Protestant as well as a Roman Catholic understanding of Scripture, flows from the triune God—the Father in election, the Son in living and dying and rising again, the Spirit in the washing of regeneration. Within Protestantism, however, disagreement comes over the point at which human involvement enters the fabric of salvation. This can be illustrated at every point of the doctrine.

Many leaders among Southern Baptists have developed an approach to salvation that accommodates this synergistic arrangement of grace. In the discussion of specific points following, this will be illustrated with references from several writings, sermons, and addresses. I will use neither names nor bibliographical location for these; my desire is not to create personal confrontation or to criticize specific individuals. My purpose is twofold: to show the pervasiveness of this idea and to illustrate the fragmenting tendency of the doctrinal position.

Grace in the Father

Many Protestants reject election as a divinely free decree and view it as a divine response to a knowledge of future human action, a less palpable but nonetheless essential synergism. Influential Southern Baptists have joined these in affirming foreknowledge as the fountain of election. "Election is based on foreknowledge," said one leader, citing 1 Peter 1:1–2. He continued by saying "God can't learn anything. . . . God knows the beginning and he knows the end, he knows the middle, he knows it all, he sees it all." He also knows that we have "a will" yet knows precisely what "you are going to do with that will." Because of this knowledge, you are "elect according to the foreknowledge of God" (1 Pet. 1:2). Foreknowledge is not a "cause," however, and thus "does not mean that God gave irresistible grace," or that believers are "part of a special elect group."

Another leader states it similarly but with some nuances of difference. "Scripture plainly teaches that predestination, which means to destine beforehand, is based on foreknowledge. God chose those whom he knew beforehand would choose him!" For scriptural foundation, he cites Romans 8:29–30 and 1 Peter 1:2 and reiterates, God elects, God predestines on the basis of knowing beforehand. That's what the word *foreknowledge* means. I've checked it out in the Greek. It just means God knows what's going to happen. On the basis that God knows, according to this, he elects.

Election, thus defined as a choice built on foreknowledge as mere prescience, intrudes human decision even into the counsels of eternity. On the one hand, it emasculates a very strong word that denotes a deliberate and rationally conceived choice ["elect"] and makes it into a mere divine capitulation to an infinite number of free choices of humans. Beyond that, or perhaps because of that capitulation, God elects by choosing not persons but a method of operation that will save as many as possible. Human freedom, sin, and the complexities of spiritual and moral growth in history impede God's desire to save all. Often quoted in support of the idea are 2 Peter 3:9 and 1 Timothy 2:4.

God knows all the hindering factors and therefore settles on a plan and method of operation that will save as many people as possible given these conditions. Grace operates not as an undeserved favor giving life to the dead but as a servant to human will. This view, held by many Baptists today, shares common ground with the Molinist theology of the Roman Catholic Jesuits. The grace of the Father arises only from precognition of human action and, thus, even in eternity "awaits" the permission of humanity to act.

This view of foreknowledge, however, viewed purely theologically and philosophically, does not achieve the "chance" for salvation for all that protagonists for the view are seeking. This kind of foreknowledge makes all things certain, but under the control of human will interjected into eternity. Second, it does not take account of the meaning of the Greek word for foreknowledge. In 2 Peter 3:17, it refers to human precognition on the basis of prophecy. In all other cases, however, it means a purpose of God established in eternity for the sake of his own pleasure and delight.

The lexicon of Bauer, Arndt, and Gingrich gives the meaning in Acts 2:23: "Of God's omniscient wisdom and intention." It translates 1 Peter 1:2, "According to the predestination of God the Father." Other translations of the same verse say, "Whom God the Father knew and chose" (Phillips); "chosen and destined by God the Father" (RSV); "whom God the Father has predestined and chosen" (Moffatt); "chosen of old in the purpose of God the Father" (NEB).

A highly influential conservative pastor preaching from Ephesians 1:4–6 described "election" as "God in His sovereignty making a choice related to salvation to be made available to human kind." Election, therefore, is "not coercive," but honors human autonomy. The sinner hearing the gospel may "freely respond"; but if "God had not chosen us," that is, made a sovereign decision to make salvation "available" to sinners, we "could not have chosen Him." Rejecting personal unconditional election as fatalism, he asserted that such a choice in eternity would mean that people are lost "because they are not elected." The same idea is present in the words of another influential pastor when he pictures election as meaning that a "child is going to hell because a child is not elect."

Election means that God exercised his sovereign prerogative beyond the desert of sinners to provide a banquet of salvation. But God's election, according to this view, does not mean that God has placed sovereign favor on one individual over any other individual. We must still choose to partake of that which God has sovereignly elected to provide. The efficacy of the Father's election, therefore, hangs on human will in time.

In a tragic and ironic twisting of the intention of divine words and actions, this view makes gracious and sovereign election the ground of hopelessness and condemnation. In reality, the New Testament makes it the only ground of hope and the certainty of salvation.

Grace in the Spirit

Some people take a view consistent with Rome in giving human cooperation a measure of efficacy in regeneration. Grace precedes, and perhaps even pre-disposes, but finally can do nothing without the permission of the human will, according to this view. Many Baptists, though professedly grace centered, have retreated from their historical and confessional view of the power of regeneration. They have adopted what is essentially Roman Catholic synergism. The grace of the Spirit who strives with the sinner must await the readiness of the human will.

Some have also turned the power of their influence against the historic view. The vigor of their denunciation and misrepresentation is remarkable. One teacher denigrated the doctrine of irresistible—that is effectual—grace by saying that "those who are going to be saved have no other option. They really don't have a choice." In addition to a belief in the sovereignty of God, he said, "Taught in the Bible also is the free will of people." After saying he had no call to reconcile God's sovereignty and man's freedom, he opted solidly for man's determining capacity. "God's grace can be resisted. People do not have to say 'yes' to the call of God, and nobody is compelled to say 'no' to the call of God."

Although he ostensibly affirmed total depravity and the necessity of the Spirit's work to lead us to repentance and faith, and that "believing is prompted by the Holy Spirit," he unreservedly asserted that "the Holy Spirit does not have to make us alive before we have this saving faith." The life of regeneration is the same as eternal life and "the New Testament is transparently clear that one believes or trusts into eternal life! It's not something that you already have! You believe into it."

Another of our representative preacher-theologians agreed wholeheartedly. Though he says a sinner could not have faith or repent unless it was granted by God, "I reject," he continues, "with all the unction, function, emotion of my soul that a man is regenerated before he believes." All sinners have received a general call from Christ who enlightens every man in the world, and the power of a call does not need to exceed that general call. Man's will normally governs the historical process. "God's will is not always done. Did you get the idea that because God is sovereign that God's will is always done?"

After mentioning rape, sodomy, and blasphemy as examples of God's sovereign rule held at bay, he stated, "No, God gave man a will, and some do perish." After showing from several Scriptures that sinners do indeed resist the Holy Spirit (e.g., Acts 7:51; Matt. 23:37), he presented irresistible grace as impersonal and coercive: "That's not love at all. I mean you become a robot. That's not love. God gives us the privilege of saying no, so that we can have the delight of saying yes to him."

Both of these energetic, highly committed spokesmen see no scriptural foundation for the doctrine of special distinguishing grace and effectual call of God. They see the new birth as following faith and point to many examples of biblical characters who resisted God's overtures to them.

It is true that instances of resistance abound. That only proves, however, the necessity of the new covenant, the Spirit's invincible operations of grace. Everything else falls short. The call of general revelation through nature does not ubdue the sinner (Rom. 1:19–21); the call of conscience does not do it (Rom. 1:28–32); the direct revelation and command of the Law does not do it (Rom. 3:19–20; 7:7–13); God's discipline and chastisement do not do it (Isa. 1:2–9; Heb. 3:7–4:2); Christ's miracles did not do it (Matt. 12:22–45; John 10:24–30); even Christ's forceful application of this pattern of rejection and his own plea cannot do it (Matt. 23:29–39); the common, though powerful operations of the Spirit, or even the undeniable evidence for the truthfulness of the spirituality of Christ's saving work cannot do it (Heb. 2:2–4; 4:4–6; 10:26–29; 1 Pet. 2:7–8; 2 Pet. 2:20–22).

In each case the fountain of unbelief and rejection is a hard, deceitful heart; a dominating predisposition to sin that has blinded the judgment of the mind and grossly corrupted the affections of the heart. Neither the absence of God's election nor the omission of the Spirit's effectual call may be blamed for the sin; human depravity sufficiently accounts for unbelief at every—even the most intense and grotesque—level of unbelief.

In addition to these examples of resistance, Scripture speaks of a call that distinguishes; it brings sinners to the submission of sorrowful repentance, joyful belief, and a hunger for righteousness. Peter contrasted those who hear the gospel and remain disobedient with a "chosen generation . . . called . . . out of darkness into his marvellous light" (1 Pet. 2:9 KJV). Paul contrasted both Jews and Greeks who see the cross as an offense or foolish to those "which are called, both Jews and Greeks" that see Christ as "the power of God, and the wisdom of God" (1 Cor. 1:24 KJV). This same effectual operation he had before him as he described himself as "a servant of Jesus Christ, called to be an apostle" (Rom. 1:1 KJV) and to the Roman Christians as "the called of Jesus Christ" (Rom. 1:6 KJV) and "called to be saints" (Rom. 1:7 KJV). He showed that he has the certainty and efficacity of this call in mind, when in Romans 8 he wrote, "For whom he did foreknow, he also did predestinate . . . whom he did predestinate, them he also called" (Rom. 8:29–30 KJV).

In accordance with this truth, Baptists have articulated the doctrine of effectual call with no hesitation. John Gano (1727–1804), the great evangelist of the Philadelphia Association, pastor of the First Baptist Church of New York, and preacher in the great revival in Kentucky, described it as "an act of sovereign grace, which flows from the everlasting love of God, and is such an irresistible impression made by the Holy Spirit upon the human soul, as to effect a blessed change."[3]

J. P. Boyce, founder and first president of the Southern Baptist Theological Seminary, noted that the external call of the gospel "meets with no success because of the willful sinfulness of man." He then added, "God knowing that this is true, not only of all mankind in general, but even of the elect whom he purposes to save in Christ, gives to these such influences of the Spirit as will lead to their acceptance of the call. This is called Effectual Calling."[4] Both of these Baptist leaders saw the call as operative through the channels of God's Word and the actions of God's providence.

This call that leads to faith differs qualitatively from all other overtures of God to sinners. It is presented in Scripture as that thing which distinguishes one sinner from another. The operations of this call culminate with the action of the Spirit in the new birth. Jesus said a person cannot even see the kingdom without the new birth, a sovereign and mysterious operation of the Spirit (John 3:8). The evidence of the Spirit's operation is belief in Christ as Savior. John already had predisposed his readers to this truth when he wrote: "But as many as received Him, to them He gave the right to become children of God, even to those who believe in His name, who were born, not of blood nor of the will of the flesh nor of the will of man, but of God" (John 1:12–13).

Paul said that our spiritual life is granted to us "even when we were dead in sins" (Eph. 2:5 KJV). He related it directly to the richness of God's mercy and the greatness of the love with which he loves us. This spiritual life, though intimately connected with eternal life, is distinguished from it. Paul drew the distinction in Romans 6:22 when he said, "But now having been freed from sin and enslaved to God, you derive your benefit, resulting in sanctification, and the outcome, eternal life." Eternal life, therefore, though connected by an unbroken chain to regeneration, is not the same thing as regeneration. Thus, the Spirit regenerates a sinner prior to faith. His faith flows from the life of regeneration; eternal life flows from faith.

As mentioned in an earlier chapter, the loss of this view of the Spirit's work has produced an increasingly decision-centered, and thus man-centered, view of salvation. This practice, now pervasive, has twisted the historic Baptist views of church membership and church discipline and created greater carnality in the churches. Views of gospel holiness have diminished accordingly. Doctrinal latitudinarianism thus meshes conveniently into the churches.

The sense of subjectivity, the autonomous self, at the heart of theological moderatism on issues of objective, propositional truth finds a soul mate in the man-centered, decision-oriented view of regeneration operative within large pockets of conservatism. Both of these find their historical Baptist warrant by the theological slant of E. Y. Mullins. He smuggled in Schleiermacher's liberal subjectivism. That liberal slant has been arrested by the reaffirmation of inerrancy, but it continues in the arena of spiritual experience.

Recovering the historic commitment to a unilateral, monergistic (as opposed to synergistic) view of grace would do much to purify both the churches and the theology. Monergism affirms that grace flows solely from divine wisdom, power, and distinguishing prerogative and is not dependent on or a response to human activity, choice, or merit. God's grace precedes not only by provision and offer, but operates with success to produce the sinner's trust in Christ.

A rediscovery of the necessity and mystery of regeneration carries purifying power in its wake. "The washing of regeneration," as Paul called it in Titus 3:5, is not baptism but the cleansing work of the Holy Spirit in his incipient saving work on the heart of enmity. Without the new birth, a person cannot see the kingdom of God; in the new birth the eyes are opened along with the heart to see and to taste the goodness of the excellence of Jesus Christ and his righteousness.

Regeneration as a gracious work of the Spirit precedes justification and produces the change of heart and perspective that eschews a person's own works for those of Christ. Better, the sinner flees from the vengeance-deserving unworthiness of his own ungodliness to gain Christ and his righteousness.

When a person is justified by faith in Christ, therefore, Scripture teaches that purifying grace both precedes and follows the faith by which sinners are justified. "Do not be deceived," Paul wrote the Corinthians. "Neither fornicators, nor idolaters, nor adulterers, nor effeminate, nor homosexuals, nor thieves, nor the covetous, nor drunkards, nor revilers, nor swindlers, shall inherit the kingdom of God" (1 Cor. 6:9–10). This is exactly what they were before hearing the gospel. Both the penalty of their sin and the polluting power of it, however, have come under the transforming power of the gospel. "Such were some of you," he was unafraid to remind them, "but you were washed, but you were sanctified, but you were justified in the name of the Lord Jesus Christ and in the Spirit of our God" (1 Cor. 6:11). Only the sovereign, effectual, transforming work of the Spirit of God in harmony with the perfect righteousness of the Savior makes such a change.

Grace in the Son

A grace-centered theology highlights not only the sovereignty of the Spirit's work, but it also rejoices in the completeness of Christ's work. The Roman Catholic view affirms the sacrificial and propitiatory aspects of the death of Jesus. Many contemporary Baptists, like Roman Catholics, view this as rendering forgiveness possible for those who take advantage of the offer. No certain effectuality, however, flows from the wounds of Christ; instead, so they say, this stream produces a reservoir of grace from which people may draw if they so choose. That is, we cannot be absolutely certain that anyone will gain salvation from the death of Christ.

As one preacher told a congregation of Baptist ministers and laymen, "In love God extended himself on the cross on behalf of every person. God in love has exhausted His every effort to make salvation available to every person." Since God has extended himself so and views every single individual from eternity with the same will to save them, "The determining issue is what do people think."

But if we cannot be certain that any sinner will actually be saved, since God already has exhausted his every effort, we can at least be sure that Christ has died for all sinners. All are loved and provided for in the same way. So strongly do some people feel about this issue of atonement that teaching its certain effectuality, in the words of one, "almost brings me to a point of righteous indignation. . . . I detest the tenet of limited atonement." This doctrine depersonalizes the gospel so the objection goes, because "you cannot look a person in the face and say to him, 'Jesus died for you.'" A person who believes in particular atonement cannot, therefore, do honest evangelism.

Not only does it stultify evangelism, in the speaker's opinion; it darkens assurance and runs roughshod over the scriptural affirmation that Christ died for the whole world and that God loves the whole world. It puts us in the hands of a very unattractive God. Strongly implied and sometimes explicitly affirmed, antagonists contend that they would not worship a God who acts in such a particularist manner. A person begins a sentence in which he is speaking of these matters with the declaration, "I don't want to serve a God who. . . ."

The multitudes of theological nuances that are problematic in these objections can be reduced to two very serious theological issues and a basic issue of biblical interpretation.

First, they assume that a sinner cannot be called on to believe the gospel unless he has immediate assurance that he is the particular object of God's saving grace. Embracing the promise of the gospel that all who believe will be saved is not enough. This panders to the self-interest of the sinner, and the evangelist as well, by shoving the presentation of the historical gospel along with its conditions and promises into a place of secondary importance. The gospel message of Christ's reconciliation, propitiation, and complete righteousness carries the promise that all who believe will be saved. We are sinners and Christ is the only hope for sinners. All who flee to him, all who want to be found in him and not in their own righteousness, will be accepted by him. This word is enough and carries the full assurance of the veracity of God himself; we are in no position to demand a knowledge of personal involvement in the saving work of Christ prior to our being called on to trust in Christ alone.

Second, they make the character of God answerable to their perceptions of the rights of man. If God does not meet our standard of fairness, if he takes sin so seriously, both original and actual, that he is determined to punish it as a demonstration of his justice in many particular instances, we feel justified in bringing him to the bar of our judgment. Such a demand amounts to rebellion and indicates that one has yet to be reconciled to God's justice in the damnation of sinners. That attitude is serious indeed, for approval of God's absolute righteousness is utterly basic to biblical faith. Though we verbalize our commitment to grace, we resent the distinguishing prerogative of divine freedom involved in the very idea. We demand that grace, God's saving purpose, be universal, or we will not accept it as genuine kindness and purely gratuitous mercy.

These objections are sinister and carry within them a justification for the sinner's rebellion against God's verdict of death. They question the legitimacy and sincerity of God's threat against Adam for disobedience.

The determining issue in biblical interpretation is, "How does Scripture represent the operations of God's saving grace?" If even one person for whom Christ has performed this work fails to receive its benefits, both the justice of God and the efficacy of Christ's work may be challenged. If, indeed, millions for whom Christ has died, perhaps even the majority, never receive the benefits he has suffered to obtain for them, how ineffective must his gracious work be? Does the Bible present grace as failing in its object?

If so, can it truly be said, "When thou shalt make his soul an offering for sin, he shall see his seed, he shall prolong his days, and the pleasure of the LORD shall prosper in his hand" (Isa. 53:10 KJV)? Did Jesus really know what he was talking about when he said, "All that the Father gives Me shall come to Me" (John 6:37)? The particularity and certainty of that confidence presents problems for the view of optional atonement when we realize how Jesus continues in his concern for those whom the Father gave Him. For those very ones whom the Father gave him he set himself apart to the cross: "For their sakes I sanctify Myself, that they themselves also may be sanctified in truth" (John 17:19).

A recovery of grace-centeredness crosses the gap from possibility to actuality. By the obedient, sacrificial shedding of his blood, Christ has wrought reconciliation, redemption, and forgiveness; and by his perfectly obedient life, he is the one in whom his people are accounted as righteous (2 Cor. 5:17–21; Rom. 4:25; 5:17–19; Gal. 3:21–25; Phil. 3:9).

Second Corinthians 5:14–15, 19, 21 is particularly significant for understanding these matters. It contains universal language, the language of effectuality, and evangelistic language. The universal language is never used outside the sphere of absolute effectuality:

> Having concluded this, that one died for all, therefore all died; and
> He died for all, so that they who live should no longer live for them-
> selves, but for Him who died and rose again on their behalf. . . . God
> was in Christ reconciling the world to Himself, not counting their

trespasses against them, and He has committed to us the word of reconciliation. . . . He made Him who knew no sin to be sin on our behalf, so that we might become the righteousness of God in Him.

All persons are under condemnation and have no possibility of doing anything to make reconciliation. If reconciliation is made, it must come through one who is qualified both in person and in work to meet the just demands of God's holiness. Only one can do that—the Lord Jesus Christ. Any who are to be reconciled will only be reconciled through him. When they are reconciled by Christ's historical death, God then at the right time and through the ordained and fitting means freely gives them all things that follow in the train of such reconciliation—regeneration, repentance, faith, justification, adoption, sanctification, perseverance, assurance, and eternal life.

On that account, the "all" (2 Cor. 5:2) for whom reconciliation is to be made will have it made by the one man Christ Jesus. When he makes that reconciliation, it counts as if they themselves had died and paid the debt due to God so that they are reconciled. "Having concluded this, that one died for all, therefore all died."

In Christ, the Father reconciled the world to himself by imputing its sins to the suitable substitute and, thus, "not counting their trespasses against them." The world, a word which means Jew and Gentile when used in the context of God's determination to save (Rom. 11:11–15; 1 John 2:2), has no ability, individually and distributively, to pay a sufficient price of reconciliation and must, therefore, be completely cared for in that once-for-all sacrifice. When it is done, it cannot be undone, nor can it be ineffectual. The price is paid, and the debt is clear. Not a one of those whose burden of payment he undertakes is omitted, "One died for all." And that "all" surely is treated as if it had paid the reconciling price on its own.

Jesus' propitiatory sacrifice has fully satisfied the wrath of God. His life has fully satisfied the law of God. Now God will be just in justifying the sinner whose sins have been cleansed; none in the whole world may be justified apart from this propitiatory work and righteous, resurrected life. As *all* who are in Adam find their connection to him effectual in being under the state of condemnation and internal corruption, so *all* who are in Christ find the work of justification effectual. The *many* in Christ is the same as the *all* in Christ (Rom. 5:12–21).

Faith, therefore, has no reality of its own apart from its object. Faith is a disposition of the mind and affections produced in conjunction with a true understanding of one's own deserved misery in sin and the supreme exclusive excellence of Christ's righteousness. The Father's pleasure in the Son, along with the display of the Son as the Savior, engenders a longing for the knowledge of him and his benefits. Faith is that act of pressing to union with Christ, the first benefit of which is justification.

Justification does not consist of inward renewal but in the imputation of Christ's own obedience. His death, purposefully embraced for the glory of God's law, procures our forgiveness; and his perfect obedience to the law constitutes justifying righteousness. Apart from this, no sinner *can ever justly be acquitted* from the verdict of eternal death. By the same token, because of his death in conformity with the Father's grace and good pleasure, sinners *certainly will be acquitted* and declared righteous.

Conclusion

When a person ignores the particularity of the grace of all three persons of the triune God, he courts theological disaster. The doctrine of universal atonement relativizes the grace of the Son in dying and suspends the operations of that grace on the thread of human will and implies the rights of man above the just prerogative of God. Levelling the operations of the Spirit to be the same with all persons, thus eliminating any doctrine of effectual calling, results in a power-impoverished Spirit pushed finally into subjection to the sinner's will. In the end, grace does not distinguish the saved from the lost but human effort, human decision, and human response. One sinner makes himself to differ from another sinner for the operations of grace must be defined as equal in every case.

Chiseling away the rough edges of the Father's particular and unconditional election into the election of precognition or the election of universal provision might relieve our sensitivities to a sense of "fair play" temporarily. The smoothed-out product, however, stands before us in humanistically refined grandeur as a most unbiblical and unattractive picture of God the holy Father and Creator/Redeemer in eternal or temporal subservience to the will of man the creature/sinner.

Reformation of Baptist identity will be unretrieved to the degree that a grace-centered theology remains unrecovered. If effectual calling cannot be reconciled with human freedom and responsibility without making a person a robot, by the same token inspiration cannot operate to produce an infallible text apart from a mindless kind of robotic dictation. If the work of salvation hangs on human will, then so must the work of revelation and inspiration. The vital organ of inerrancy cannot survive in the absence of the nutrition of grace.

Chapter 8

Trinitarian Christ-Centered Theology

Fundamentally Trinitarian

Baptist commitment to proclamation and instruction stands in need of a conscientious and purposeful orientation toward a fully trinitarian doctrine of divine revelation and salvation. In its exposition of the Confession of Faith, the Philadelphia Association asserted that the article on the Trinity is a "cornerstone in the Christian faith" and that without it "the whole superstructure will fall."[1] That position assuredly represents the biblical viewpoint.

Following out the great acts of the Divine Being as presented in Scripture leads to an irreducible conviction that the Father, the Son, and the Holy Spirit operate as distinct persons with appropriate and often discreet functions. The activity of each, however, so conforms to the single intention of God that the whole of any of the acts may be said to be the work of the one God. So it is with creation, providence, and redemption.

Our knowledge of and reconciliation to this triune God, however, most specifically involve the work of Christ Jesus, the Son. The Father determines that the work shall be done, elects individuals to salvation and gives them to the Son, and arranges for the effectual completion of it. Most critically, however, and arising from the intrinsic necessity of the entire redemptive transaction, the Father has sent the Son as the fullest revelation of God and as the one in whose work redemption consists.

The Holy Spirit, sharing all the essential attributes of deity, fully knowledge-able of the eternal relation between Father and Son, and himself the stream through whom the love and knowledge of Father and Son are reciprocated, takes the part of sealing to the elect every aspect of the redemption accomplished by Christ (Eph. 1:1–14).

Scripture unfolds this beautiful trinitarian arrangement in passage after pas-sage. Jesus told his disciples, "When the Helper comes, whom I will send to you from the Father, that is the Spirit of truth, who proceeds from the Father, He will testify about of Me" (John 15:26). To the Galatians Paul wrote, "Because you are sons, God has sent forth the Spirit of His Son into our hearts, crying 'Abba! Father!'" (Gal. 4:6). Later in the book of Ephesians, Paul summed up a statement on Christ's reconciling work with the observation, "For through Him we both have our access in one Spirit to the Father" (Eph. 2:18).

Closing up a dense treatment of the revelation of God's eternal purpose which culminates in Christ, Paul penned his earnest prayer, "For this reason, I bow my knees before the Father, from whom every family in heaven and on earth derives its name, that He would grant you, according to the riches of His glory, to be strengthened with power through His Spirit in the inner man; so that Christ may dwell in your hearts through faith; and that you, being rooted and grounded in love, may be able to comprehend with all the saints what is the breadth and length and height and depth, and to know the love of Christ which surpasses knowledge, that you may be filled up to all the fulness of God" (Eph. 3:14–19).

This marvelous passage points to several fundamental aspects of trinitarian reality.

First, all structures of authority derive their arrangement from the internal relations of the Trinity with the assumption of the priority of the Father, not in essence, but in recognition of personal distinction.

Second, the Spirit communicates the "riches of His glory" to and within the "inner man." Both from a Godward and manward standpoint, only the Divine Being can do this. To reach the inner man with power, impressing upon it the riches of the Father's glory, is the operation of a divine person. The Spirit in his immediate operation on the soul entices and inflames it with a compelling sense and taste of the Father's glory.

Third, in doing this the mysterious effect is that Christ dwells in our hearts by faith. The internal strengthening by the Spirit in accord with the Father's glory opens to us a knowledge of the love of Christ which contains within it all the fullness of God. This rich and ineffable trinitarianism finally distills into human experience, in both knowledge and redemption, as fully manifest by faith in Jesus Christ.

If we do not purposefully pursue a trinitarian discussion of every aspect of God's merciful action toward us, we are untrue to Scripture and forfeit that which is specifically Christian in the revealed redemptive scheme. Each person of the triune God has interest in every aspect of Christian truth and experience.[2]

Apart, however, from the incarnation and redemptive work of God the Son, we would have no knowledge of God as either triune or filled with mercy and loving-kindness. "No one has seen God at any time," John reminds us; "the only begotten Son, who is in the bosom of the Father, He has explained Him" (John 1:18). John the Baptist (if we take the verses to be a part of his sermon) affirms that true knowledge of God, and redemption rests in the work of the Son:

> For He whom God has sent speaks the words of God; for He
> gives the Spirit without measure. The Father loves the Son, and has
> given all things into His hand. He who believes in the Son has eternal
> life; but he who does not obey the Son shall not see life, but the wrath
> of God abides on him. (John 3:34–36)

The Son, sent into the world and, in his incarnation, recipient of the Spirit without measure, speaks the words of God. In fact, he manifests in his person the glory of Son, and the fullness of the Godhead dwells in him in bodily form. Because of the infinite and eternal love of the Father for the Son, which love forms the bond of essential union between them, he commits the entire process of redemption, judgment, and glorious consummation into the hands of the Son. None will have eternal life who does not see that eternal life abides specifically in the work and words of Jesus, Son of God and Son of Man in one person.

Fuller's Confrontation with Socinianism

An example of the importance of maintaining a Christ-centered emphasis on the Trinity may be seen in Andrew Fuller's opposition to Socinianism. This system of religious thought denied the deity of Christ and consequently the

Trinity, the Fall, and consequently original sin, the atoning work of Christ, and consequently justification by faith. Though he could well have engaged in face-to-face theological polemics, Fuller sought to answer the Socinians' claim that their virtue, built on rationality, was greater than that of the "Calvinists."

Fuller's approach at refutation focused on the moral tendencies of Socinianism, particularly in regard to those states of mind and heart that are supposed to be the outflow of Christian truth. Fuller examined such subjects as the conversion of profligates, the conversion of professed unbelievers (such as Jews, the heathen, and "Mahometans"), the standard of morality, love for God, candor and benevolence, humility, accusations of lack of charity and indulgence in bigotry, love for Christ, veneration for the Scriptures, cheerfulness of mind, and motives to gratitude, obedience, and heavenly mindedness. With his characteristic theological alacrity, Fuller showed how the Socinian scheme diminished at every point the effects that the Bible attributes to Christian faith.

Fuller's powerful application of the superiority of Christian orthodoxy to Socinian ideas in evoking the highest and holiest human response in each area under discussion has an overwhelming cumulative effect. In each point, Christ's essential deity stands either directly or by implication as the substantive issue. For the conversion of profligates Fuller observed that if "faith towards our Lord Jesus Christ is another essential part of true conversion," Socinian principles are "unadapted to induce us to trust in Christ" but conversely "turn off our attention and affection from him." Fuller contended that we might as well expect "figs of thistles" as to expect "repentance towards God, or faith towards our Lord Jesus Christ, proceeding from Socinian principles."[3]

Socinian writers, Fuller pointed out, "cannot so much as *pretend* that their doctrine has been used to convert profligate sinners to the love of God and holiness."[4] On the other hand, conversions to Christ from among the meanest parts of society resulting in joy and holiness and worship of God came in massive proportions from those who preached what the Socinians oppose. "It is well known," Fuller insisted, "what sort of preaching it was that produced such great effects in many nations of Europe, about the time of the Reformation."

> Whatever different sentiments were professed by the Reformers, I suppose they were so far agreed, that the doctrines of human depravity, the Deity and atonement of Christ, justification by faith, and sanctification by the influence of the Holy Spirit, were the great topics of their ministry.[5]

This doctrinal orientation served not only the Reformation but the Puritans such as Perkins, Gouge, and Bunyan, and the preachers of the First Great Awakening in America such as Edwards and Tennent, and even now [ca. 1792] was bearing fruit in "Virginia, the Carolinas, and Georgia."[6]

Does orthodoxy produce charity toward others? Since, according to Fuller, he could not "acknowledge as Christians" those who rejected doctrines "essential to Christianity," he was accused of spiritual pride, bigotry, and uncharitableness. Fuller, in light of this, determined to answer this question: "Whether as believing in the Deity and atonement of Christ, with other correspondent doctrines, we be required, by the charity inculcated in the gospel, to acknowledge, as fellow Christians those who thoroughly and avowedly reject them."[7]

Fuller argued cogently and powerfully that Christian conviction is neither bigoted nor uncharitable. A bigot maintains preference for one's own opinions in spite of evidence and judges all others in light of those personal opinions so maintained. Speaking truthfully as required by divine revelation cannot be identified with that attitude. Speaking the truth for the sake of love to it and Christ and acting with discernment in light of that truth has no relation to bigotry. No person "who is open to conviction can be a bigot, whatever be his religious sentiments."

The Socinian position implied a severe and dangerous flaw in Christian worship. If the Socinians were right, then Christians were "habitual idolators." But if the "proper Deity of Christ be a Divine truth," then all of those aspects of Christian faith that depend on acknowledging his deity cannot be true of Socinians; the conclusion, therefore, is "Socinians would not have been acknowledged by the apostle Paul, as true Christians." "If we believe," Fuller continued with bulldog tenacity, "the Deity and atonement of Christ to be essential to Christianity, we must necessarily think those who reject these doctrines to be no Christians; nor is it inconsistent with charity to speak accordingly."[8]

Failure to grasp the importance of Christ and his deity means a failure in every distinguishing aspect of Christian faith. "Take away Christ," Fuller reasoned, and then stated more specifically,

> nay, take away the Deity and atonement of Christ; and the whole ceremonial of the Old Testament appears to us little more than a dead mass of uninteresting matter: prophecy loses all that is interesting and endearing; the gospel is annihilated, or ceases to be that *good news* to

lost sinners which it professes to be, practical religion is divested of its most powerful motives, the evangelical dispensation of its peculiar glory, and heaven itself of its most transporting joys.[9]

Christ in Preaching

The power of a Christ-centered theology materializes in Christ-centered preaching. Christ-centered preaching vibrates with intense spiritual power, for the special operation of the Holy Spirit is precisely this: "He shall glorify Me, for He will take of Mine and will disclose it to you" (John 16:14). Nothing in Scripture can be cast aside as disconnected from the whole. All of it is relevant to its ultimate purpose described in Hebrews 1:1–3:

> Having already spoken at many times and through many means in past times through the prophets, God spoke in these last days through a Son whom he appointed heir of all things, through whom also he made the world; who, being the effulgence of his glory and the exact impression of his person, and upholding all things through the word of his power, and having made purification of sins, sat down at the right hand of the majesty on high [author's translation].

All events and revelation of the Old Testament were driving toward unfolding the meaning of the final redemptive work of Jesus Christ. Christ, therefore, in saving his people is the center of biblical revelation.

No greater evidence of the intensity of power resonant in the proclamation of Christ, precisely with the conviction of his essentiality and effectuality in saving sinners, can be found than in the sermons of Charles Spurgeon. His focus on Christ reflected his mature grasp of the nature of biblical revelation as moving with greater and greater clarity toward the incarnation and the redemptive work of Christ. One would search in vain for a sermon from Spurgeon in which he does not exalt Christ.

On August 3, 1890, Spurgeon preached from Daniel 10:11, "O Daniel, a man greatly beloved" (KJV). After showing the effect of Daniel's confidence in the love of God toward him, Spurgeon applied this same surety to the work of Christ for his people. He has loved them with an everlasting love and has redeemed them by his blood.

Thy God took upon himself thy nature, and on the cross he bore thy sins in his own body on the tree. The chastisement of thy peace was upon him, and with his stripes thou art healed. The bloodmark is on thee now; thou art one for whom he died in that special way which secures effectual salvation to thee. He loved his church, and gave himself for it; and this is the song of that church in heaven, "Thou has [sic] redeemed us to God by thy blood out of every kindred, and tongue, and people, and nation; and hast made us unto our God kings and priests: and we shall reign on the earth." If thou hast been redeemed by the precious blood of Jesus, verily, I say unto thee, thou art "a man greatly beloved."[10]

Not only late but early in his ministry, Spurgeon had this Christological focus. The first entry of the first *Sword and Trowel*, "What Shall Be Done for Jesus," speaks of the manifold ways in which the eternal Father has honored Jesus. Every blessing the Father grants us comes only through "the man Christ Jesus." He incarnates every office that effects reconciliation with God—that is, prophet, priest, and king. Literally thousands of times we read Spurgeon's affirmations of the orthodox view of Christ as God and man in one person.

"What can ye conceive," Spurgeon exclaimed, "of splendour blazing around the throne of the Most High, which will not also be seen gleaming with equal refulgence from the seat of him who is 'God over all blessed for ever?' It is with no trembling lip that we sing *his* praise." Spurgeon stated it as a settled principle that "you cannot taste the sweetness of any *doctrine* till you have remembered Christ's connection with it."[11] Six years earlier, 1859, in a sermon entitled "Christ Precious to Believers," Spurgeon declared:

Election is a good thing; to be chosen of God, and precious; but we are elect in Christ Jesus. Adoption is a good thing; . . . ay, but we are adopted in Christ Jesus and made joint-heirs with him. Pardon is a good thing—who will not say so?—ay, but we are pardoned through the precious blood of Jesus. Justification—is not that a noble thing, to be robed about with a perfect righteousness?—ay, but we are justified in Jesus. To be preserved—is not that a precious thing?—ay; but we are preserved in Christ Jesus, and kept by his power even to the end. Perfection—who shall say that this is not precious? But he hath raised us up and made us sit together with him in heavenly places in Jesus Christ—so that Christ must be good positively, for he is all the best things in one.[12]

Not only doctrine but the knowledge of God himself inextricably involves the reality of Christ and him crucified. In January 1855, Spurgeon preached, marking the changing date on earth, on the "Immutability of God." The contemplation of Christ leads into a fullness in the contemplation of God.

> The most excellent study for expanding the soul, is the science of Christ, and him crucified, and the knowledge of the Godhead in the glorious Trinity. Nothing will so enlarge the intellect, nothing so mag-nify the whole soul of man, as a devout, earnest, continued investiga-tion of the great subject of the Deity. And, whilst humbling and expanding, this subject is eminently *consolatory*. Oh, there is, in con-templating Christ, a balm for every wound, in musing on the Father there is a quietus for every grief; and in the influence of the Holy Ghost, there is a balsam for every sore. Would you lose your sorrows? Would you drown your cares? Then go, plunge yourself in the Godhead's deepest sea; be lost in his immensity; and you shall come forth as from a couch of rest, refreshed and invigorated. I know noth-ing which can so comfort the soul; so calm the swelling billows of grief and sorrow; so speak peace to the winds of trial, as a devout musing upon the subject of the Godhead. It is to that subject I invite you this morning.[13]

They Have Hid My Lord

In the conflict of 1770 that gave rise to the small beginnings of the New Connection of General Baptists, Gilbert Boyce, apparently with a spirit of deep sincerity, sought to convince Dan Taylor to abstain from schism. To do so, he knew that he must convince Taylor that the deity of Christ and the doctrine of the Trinity should not be divisive among General Baptist ranks. Since we believe in the most important doctrine, Boyce reminded Taylor, of the unity, self-existence, and infinite perfection of God, why should we separate from one another? True, you believe in the deity of Christ and that in some way three separate persons each holding the full essence of deity constitute this one self-existent God, and I do not,

Boyce averred, but what is that among so many other grand and august truths on which we agree?

Taylor responded by continuing his efforts to establish a doctrinally sound witness through the churches. The confession which defined the distinctives of the New Connection stated, "We believe, that our Lord Jesus Christ is God and man, united in one person: or possessed of divine perfections united to human nature, in a way which we pretend not to explain, but think ourselves bound by the word of God firmly to believe."[14]

One hundred years later, J. C. Means, an Old Connection Baptist minister, analyzed why that group was dying and on the verge of extinction while the "orthodox brethren," the churches of the New Connection, were thriving.[15] "Their churches," Means observed, "are pervaded by an earnest and devout feeling in which we are conscious that our own churches are deficient." In addition, "their services excite a warm interest which ours fail to kindle," and their "missions attain to a degree of success which ours cannot reach, if indeed we make any missionary efforts at all." Why was this true? In an amazing display of theological confusion, Means pleaded for a recovery of all the effects of orthodoxy while still screening out the substance of it. Particularly grotesque is his call for devotion to Christ.

> We have talked about the Saviour, discussed his claims to our reverence, and retrenched the honours which, as we thought, were unduly ascribed to Him, till, I fear, we have too often come unconsciously to look upon Him rather as the subject of our arguments than the object of our trust; and have been more anxious to guard against making too much of Him than fearful of making too little. We have failed, I am afraid, to enthrone Him in our hearts as the Son of God; to make His work and teaching the ground of our highest hopes and purest affections; to commune with Him closely and constantly, till we could say with Paul, "The life which I now live in the flesh, I live by the faith of the Son of God, who loved me, and gave himself for me."

Means wanted to have piety without an object of worship, devotion with nothing to inspire it, repentance without any conviction concerning the origin of sin. "What is required," giving a sham of definiteness to his confusion, "is belief in Christ, not belief about Him." Faith, very conveniently, "did not mean orthodoxy" to the apostles of the first century. The connection between faith and salvation is "not the award of deliverance from hell to the holders of a creed," but a process of purification of soul. Living conviction makes the difference. The extent and completeness of purification "will depend on the presence and intensity of the conviction by which it is worked out—that is, on the power of faith."

So lay aside the "dogmatic forms" and the "needless and erroneous definitions" for more suitable forms, but if we want to "gain the ear of men" and "touch their hearts," we must maintain the "vital power of those truths." Only in that way will anyone be convinced that "salvation is offered him through faith in Jesus as his saviour."

Surely the insipid condition of the Old Connection and their slump to virtual extinction should have taught Means that intensity of devotion apart from the intrinsic worthiness of the object has no value at all. Means wanted a religion of human conviction, faith, devotion, piety, and righteousness without a corresponding truth to be believed, worthy object of trust, or sufficient redemptive transaction. In Means's view, a Christ who is not God is to be enthroned in our hearts. His work and teaching, which is that of a mere creature, should be the "ground of our highest hopes and purest affections." We are to commune with him who is merely a departed saint.

Conclusion

Fuller was right. The loss of Christ, as viewed through his essential deity and truly substitutionary atonement, means the loss of Christianity's most "powerful motives," its "peculiar glory," and its "most transporting joys." Preaching that fails to crystalize its message into the person and work of Christ falls short of being a truly biblical message. The maintenance and propagation of truth, power, joy, forgiveness—the gospel—falls limply to the ground apart from a Christ-centered understanding of the Trinity. Means also knew it; but the journey back was too far.

Chapter 9

Theologically Integrated Ecclesiology

Building the Church on the Whole Truth

Baptist ecclesiology has been the product of a vigorous application of the full range of orthodox and evangelical theology to Christ's purpose to build his church. Christ promised to build his church on the confession of Peter at Caesarea Philippi in Matthew 16. When Peter said, "Thou art the Christ, the Son of the living God" (Matt. 16:16 KJV), he made a statement pregnant with massive *theological* implications concerning the nature of God and the nature of Christ.

When Jesus told Peter that flesh and blood had not revealed this to him but the Father in heaven, he made a statement full of *experiential* implications for the nature of human faith. When Jesus began immediately to tell his disciples of his impending death and resurrection (Matt. 16:21), he insisted that his messiahship and the Father's call to faith could not find full expression apart from his atoning work. The doctrine of the church, therefore, cannot stand as an isolated item discussed blandly and disconnectedly as a Baptist "distinctive," somehow self-existent and independent of other theological concerns.

As R. Albert Mohler Jr. has suggested in *Beyond the Impasse*, "Baptist 'distinctives' must be interpreted in terms of a larger and more comprehensive continuity with the larger Christian tradition." Baptist consent to the "orthodox tradition" as channeled through "Nicaea, Chalcedon, Augustine, Luther, Calvin, and the Protestant confessions" may be seen in the "sturdy confessional tradition of Baptists developed over four centuries."[1]

Timothy George in this same book also argues for a Baptist identity in dialogue with evangelicalism in the present and the confessional fullness of the past. He contends that we must be aware that heresy exists and is destructive of Christian life. Affirming Mohler's call for "theological triage," George recommends that "theological discrimination is a necessity." Prioritizing doctrinal issues for recovery on the one hand and fellowship on the other must be pursued with wisdom, sensitivity, and careful biblical reflection. Moving his discussion to one specific doctrinal issue begging for honest interaction, George indicates that resurgent Calvinism must win confidence by dispelling any fears that errors of the past or current caricatures justify exclusion from the Baptist recovery.

Although George does not mention the scenario, Calvinists could just as easily ask for their own set of assurances from the non-Calvinists; that is, will their Arminianism lead again into liberalism, Socinianism, shallow decisionistic evangelism that fills God's churches with the worldly, and a theological downgrade to open theism. George advocates the "cultivation of a holistic orthodoxy" as a necessity. The type of transformation needed in Baptist life, specifically "denominational life," calls for "nothing less than a theological revival, something of more substance than 'a happy hour with Jesus.'"[2]

Walter Shurden would see such calls for theological muscle as the "debaptistification" of Baptist churches. He would prefer to see Baptist identity as a manifestation of and the zealous protection of individual autonomy in matters of faith. A portion of that clearly is within the Baptist heritage but not separate from the context of a greater body of biblical doctrine. Shurden's sort of historical truncation of Baptist identity not only fails in its grasp of the doctrinal history of Baptists but disfigures Baptist ecclesiology by severing it from the complete life of faith.

Any attempt to isolate the doctrine of the church, or even a narrow and singular aspect of it, from the remainder of divine revelation invents a lonely and lifeless shell in the place of an organism that in reality is seamlessly woven to the whole of biblical truth. The church has the status of the body of Christ seen clearly in Ephesians 1:22–23 and 5:23 and Colossians 1:18. Right understanding of Christ in full expression of deity and humanity in one person (Col. 1:15–20), his effectual sacrifice to reconcile his people and make them subject to him

(Eph. 1:15–23; Col. 1:20–23), his eternal relation of love to the Father (Col. 1:13, 19), regeneration by the Holy Spirit—all these truths and more—have immediate impact on one's doctrine of the church.

If indeed the church is the body of Christ and not of human origin or susceptible to autonomous human redefinition, then the doctrine of the church must emerge from its organic relation with the whole of Christian doctrine. Paul affirms that the entire revelation of the mystery of God was committed to the apostles and prophets in order that through the church the manifold wisdom of God might be made known.

> To me, the very least of all saints, this grace was given, to preach to the Gentiles the unfathomable riches of Christ, and to bring to light what is the administration of the mystery which for ages has been hidden in God who created all things; so that the manifold wisdom of God might now be made known through the church to the rulers and the authorities in the heavenly places. (Eph. 3:8–10)

John Spilsbury (1593–1668) promoted a definition of faith, as well as a profession of faith, that involves a large amount of Christ-centered theological content. Saving faith, or confession of Christ, requires that men "confesse him in his Name and Titles that his Father hath honoured him with, and set him out by." Spilsbury argued not only that saving faith arises from a biblically sound Christology, but that it involves personal submission to the views of baptism and church institution that were argued so strongly by the early Particular Baptists.

> [Christ is] a sufficient and onely Saviour; and the Mediatour of the new Testament; as King, Priest, and Prophet. A Priest to redeeme and purchase his people; a Prophet to teach and instruct that people; and a King to protect and defend the said people in their obedience to the truth, revealed by him as a Prophet, and by him as a King commanded to be obeyed. And as this is to be knowne and believed of such as expect life by him: even so it is to be confessed, by a professed subjection to him in the same. The Rule of which professed subjection and confession, is the instituted order and administration of Christs Testament, for no other confession doth he approve of, but that which holds him forth to be Jesus Christ, the Sonne of God, come in the flesh, dead, and risen againe, ascended, and exalted at Gods right hand,

to the throne of his Father *David*; and so to be Lord of Lords, and King of Kings. And submission to the instituted order and administration of Christs Testament, is an ordained confession of this believing in him, in a professed subjection to him. This confession doth Christ therefore require of such as believe in him, and ownes no believing unto salvation in his new Testament, once confirmed by his death, where this is refused. For the benefits of Christ as Mediatour, and his administration, and the state, order, and rules of that Testament whereof he is Mediatour, and the subjects partaking of those benefits, goe together in the record of Scripture; so that if there be no baptizing into Christ, then is there not confession of Christ, according to his appointment, . . . And if not confession of Christ, according to his appointment, then no faith to salvation, by Christ expresly owned.[3]

A strong case can be made that he is right on the Christological aspect of the confession but that his identification of saving confession with baptism does not enjoy the same iron-clad certainty of the former. Ecclesiological error is not necessarily perilous; Christological error certainly is. Spilsbury's contention, however, that a biblical doctrine of the church must include an orthodox view of the person of Christ and an evangelical view of his work is certainly right. If his limitation of saving faith to those who also follow in believer's baptism cuts too narrowly, his argument that the witness of baptism assumes such a confession must still be taken seriously and argues strongly for a Baptist understanding of the church. Baptism, apart from the belief and confession of saving truth, is empty whether it be of an infant or an adult.

In the spirit of this theologically integrated ecclesiology, Oliver Hart (1723–1795) preached and published his sermon, *A Gospel Church Portrayed and Her Orderly Service Pointed Out,* to the Philadelphia Association. After demonstrating through metaphors how all of its parts fit together, applying a New Testament fulfillment to 2 Chronicles 29:35, and how each part is a picture of the mercy of God to his people, Hart summarized the God-centered theological emphasis of his discussion.

> Having thus attempted to describe the house of the Lord, as built upon the gospel plan; perhaps some may expect, that something should be said respecting the *architect.* When we see a magnificent edifice, neatly executed according to the rules of art, we are naturally led to

inquire, Who was the builder? To this . . . I might return a summary answer. "He that built all things is God." But the apostle addressing the Corinthian church, is more explicit. "Ye are God's building." Yes. The triune Jehovah was the builder of this edifice. God, the Father, chose the materials: God, the Son, purchased them with his most precious blood; and God the Holy Ghost, by his powerful and gracious influences, hews, planes, polishes and fits them for the building. Each of these divine persons is equally concerned in the erection of the house. Jehovah then is the grand Architect or Master Builder; therefore we have no reason to wonder that it is such a magnificent structure.[4]

Neither reductionism nor minimalism in ecclesiology will satisfy the saints of God. Too much is at stake. The "unfathomable riches of Christ" as well as the "manifold wisdom of God" find demonstration in the church. We must be determined, therefore, that the mind, heart, and corporate fellowship increasingly reflect the truth of God in all its fullness. I will seek to demonstrate briefly how Baptists historically have sought to achieve this full expression of divine truth in the church by looking at only three elements: membership, the eldership, and discipline.

Membership

Such desires drove early Baptists in their formation of churches. Benjamin Keach wrote a work entitled *The Glory of a True Church and its Discipline Display'd* in 1697. He defined a church like this:

> A church of Christ, according to the Gospel-Institution, is a Congregation of Godly Christians, who as a Stated-Assembly (being first baptized upon the Profession of Faith) do by mutual agreement and consent give themselves unto the Lord, and one to another, according to the Will of God; and do ordinarily meet together in one Place, for the Publick Service and Worship of God; among whom the Word of God and Sacraments are duly administred, according to Christ's Institution.[5]

The members of this church "must declare to the Church . . . what God hath done for their souls, or their Experiences of a Saving work of Grace upon their

Hearts, and also the Church should enquire after, and take full satisfaction concerning their Holy Lives, or Good Conversations."

The Charleston Association, established in 1751, called for a knowledge not only "of themselves and of their lost state by nature, and of the way of salvation by Christ," but also affirmed a number of other doctrinal issues desirable in church members. They should have

> some degree of knowledge of God in his nature, perfections, and works; and of Christ in his person as the son of God; of his proper deity; of of [sic] his incarnation; of his offices, as prophet, priest and king; of justification by his righteousness; pardon by his blood; satisfaction by his sacrifice; and of his prevalent intercession; And also of the spirit of God; his person, offices and operations; and of the important truths of the gospel, and doctrines of grace; or how otherwise should the church be the *pillar and ground of truth?*[6]

Richard Furman (1755–1825) discussed both the universal church and the local church. The former is known perfectly only to God to whom the "real and the apparent are the same." It is bound to Christ by a threefold cord: covenantal, because he has acted for them in the covenant of redemption; natural, because he has taken their nature; and vital, because he has given them his Spirit. This church is a habitation of God through the Spirit, the "pillar and ground of the truth," and the means of "displaying the sovereign and free grace of God to all rational creatures."[7]

The local worshipping assembly Furman described as a "society of faithful men, to whom the word of God is purely preached and the ordinances duly administered and which frequently assembles together, to unite in acts of social worship." The members must be those who, as far as human judgment can ascertain, have repented toward God and placed faith in Christ, have "supreme love toward God," are subject to his authority and government, maintain an "open profession of His Name," and show a zealous "concern for the honor of the divine majesty" as well as an "unshaken attachment to his cause, interest and people."[8]

Even constituting the membership of the church, therefore, calls for clear apprehension of several elements of experiential doctrine. "They must be truly gracious persons" in the words of the *Summary of Church Discipline of the Charleston Association*. That is, "none are fit materials of a gospel church, without having first experienced an entire change of nature." In what capacity does the applicant see himself as receiving Christ? What are his basic understandings of Christ's person and work, and how does he think and feel that these truths relate to him?

J. P. Boyce gave the necessary reminder that "many members are as yet babes in Christ, and therefore, not prepared to express that knowledge of the doctrine of the word to be expected of those who are teachers." He continued, however, "If an applicant for membership gives evidence of a change of heart and is so far convinced of the truth of these peculiarities which mark us as a denomination as to desire to unite with us, he should be admitted." He still tied membership to doctrinal and experiential qualifications. He probably had in mind those doctrinal matters mentioned above by the Charleston Association's *Manual of Discipline*. No member should disturb the church with any contradictions until by "thorough examination of the Scriptures he has satisfied himself that the church is in error."[9]

If a member should draw the conclusion that the church is in error, he should seek a formal audience with the eldership and doctrinally mature church members. In the context of such a discussion, three courses of action are possible. He might convince the leadership of his view and gain a change in the church's position; he might choose to remain in spite of the difference by agreeing to hold his view privately and not disturb the church further with it (this assumes, of course, that in conscience he is able to consider it *adiaphora*); he might leave amicably without incurring censure and join a congregation more consistent with his studied viewpoint.

Should such a member, however, insist on staying while openly resisting the confession of the church, he makes himself liable to the discipline of the church, if he will not be corrected with gentleness (2 Tim. 2:25). "Reject a factious man after a first and second warning, knowing that such a man is perverted and is sinning, being self-condemned" (Titus 3:10–11). "If anyone does not obey our instruction in this letter, take special note of that person and do not associate with him, so that he will be put to shame. Yet do not regard him as an enemy, but admonish him as a brother" (2 Thess. 3:14–15).

Those who examine candidates for membership, however, must have a clear and unwavering grasp of the doctrinal issues involved and their pertinence to conversion as well as the subject's experience and expression of it. What is the nature of regeneration, and how would we expect its reality to be operative and evident in the demeanor and testimony of a person desiring church membership? The minister in particular, but the other members of the congregation in general, must have insight into these fundamental aspects of Christian truth and experience. He must have enough doctrinal maturity also to know when he may proceed from a judgment of charity and when he should ask for further counsel in expectation of obtaining a clearer witness to the saving experience. From its inception, the very constitution of the church and the future of its spiritual vitality depend on the most careful spiritual understanding and application of orthodox evangelical Christianity.

Eldership

If such is true of the membership, what of those who are the biblically ordained teachers of the church and proclaimers of its message to an unbelieving world? In his *Three Changes in Theological Institutions,* J. P. Boyce asserted a greatly increased responsibility for the doctrinal maturity of the minister and related this task to the other concerning membership.

> While, however, this is all that should be required of a member of the church, we should ask of one of its ministers such an agreement to its expressed doctrine as should be even more than substantial. The points of difference here allowable are very trivial, being such as will not in any respect interfere in his ministrations with that fullness of agreement of Scripture truth, through which he is enabled to preach the word of God without danger of misleading his people in any particular.[10]

In a section entitled "Of the Work of a Pastor, Bishop, or Overseer," Keach outlined the doctrine-centeredness of pastoral ministry. As one who rightly divides the word of truth as a steward of the mysteries of the gospel, the pastor must be a man of "good understanding and experience." He must be sound in the faith, acquainted with the mysteries of the gospel, "faithful and skilful to declare the Mind of God" because God has committed to him the ministry of reconciliation. Given all that is involved in reconciliation, Keach asked, "What interest hath God greater in the World which he hath committed unto men than this?" In addition, "he must make known the whole Counsel of God to the People."[11]

William Rogers (1751–1824), Baptist minister in Philadelphia and professor of English at the University of Pennsylvania, found in Oliver Hart the quintessence of a Christian minister. When he preached a memorial sermon for Hart in 1795, he spoke of him as a "Minister of the everlasting Gospel." As such, the object of his study should be the attributes and perfections of Jehovah, the creation, fall and recovery of man, and the incarnation and passion of Christ as a manifestation of the everlasting love of God.

In summary, the minister must embrace and be apt to teach all the doctrines of the Bible such as "salvation by free and sovereign grace, justification by imputed righteousness, repentance for and remission of sin, regeneration, sanctification by the Holy Spirit, adoption into the family of God, the final perseverance of the Saints, together with every other revealed truth and enjoined duty."

In light of the infinite price by which the souls of God's sheep are bought, nothing should concern the gospel minister more than the clear proclamation of these truths by which Jehovah's ineffable condescension to save sinners is set forth.[12]

Richard Furman (1755–1825), protégé of Oliver Hart and his successor at the First Baptist Church of Charleston, also believed that deep doctrinal obligations rested on the pastor. A large portion of his description of the constitution of the church focused on the ministry of the pastor. Furman's high view of Scripture along with his thorough commitment to the necessity of a divine revelation led him to impute immense importance to the teaching task of the preacher. Both a clear understanding of doctrine and a true acquaintance with "experimental religion" are needed to carry out the pastoral charge faithfully.

> It is necessary, therefore, that the bishop, or pastor, be well instructed in the sacred doctrines of the gospel: Concerning the nature and perfections of the Deity; the person and offices of Christ, and salvation through him; the influence and operation of the divine spirit; and the nature of grace and holiness: In a word of whatever is essential to salvation. Especially, he should be truly acquainted with experimental religion, and deeply affected with its reality and importance.[13]

"Experimental religion" formed the center of pastoral concern for the old Baptists as well as the Puritans. This phrase incorporated the conviction that the purpose of life is to know God and enjoy him forever. Everything that God has revealed to us should increase the depth of our repentance, the intensity of our love for God, the undefiled character of our devotion, the expansiveness of our gratitude for his grace, the determination of our wills to see the Lord glorified, the purity of our zeal for holiness, a holy dissatisfaction with the level of our knowledge of God, and our boldness for the propagation of the gospel. "How shall we, that are dead to sin, live any longer therein!" (Rom. 6:2 KJV).

Meditation, prayer, right motives, right spirit, holy fervor—an incorporation of truth into the very soul—must all precede and gush forth in the task of preaching, for the preacher must "send forth all his soul." Furman described the experimental application of doctrine as the most compelling task of the preacher.

> Here again he must distinguish between the law and gospel; and between the characters of men, as saints or sinners: Must point out the ruined and guilty state of all by nature, under the curse of a broken law; sound, as it were, Mount Sinai's thunder in the sinner's ear; present the flaming mountain to his eye; and thus produce the awful evidence, to that momentous truth, "that by the deeds of the law, shall no flesh living be justified." To the humbled sinner, and believing soul, he must describe Jesus, as "the Lamb of God, who taketh away the sins of the world:" As the only, the almighty, and the willing savior. He must describe him, in his person, his offices, his works of love and grace, his bleeding passion, and triumphant state. He must open, as it were, Immanuel's heart, in the description of divine compassion, and publish the gracious invitation of the gospel, to perishing and heavy laden souls; must show the abundant grace in the promises, and the foundation on which faith may rest, in the faithfulness, infinite goodness, sovereign mercy, and unchangeable purpose of the promiser. To him, belongs the important work of drawing aside the veil of time, and opening the awful scenes of eternity, on his hearers minds: Of describing the joys of paradise; and the terrors of the infernal world. To present man with the humbling scenes of his mortality; and erect the throne of decisive judgment in his mental view.[14]

This scene of preaching depicted by Furman was what W. B. Johnson called "speaking the word of the Lord from the experience of its power."[15]

Discipline

Church discipline is the third element that demonstrates the indissoluble ties between ecclesiology and doctrine. Paul told the Thessalonians, "Now we command you, brothers, in the name of our Lord Jesus Christ, that you separate yourselves from every brother conducting himself in a disorderly manner and not according to the tradition which you received from us" (2 Thess. 3:6, author's translation). "Tradition" is the same word used in 2:15 where Paul admonished them "to stand firm and hold fast the *traditions* you have been taught whether through word or through a letter from us" (author's translation). Matthew 15 (three times) and Mark 7 (five times) record Jesus's use of this word in a negative sense.

These uses refer to specific teachings of the Pharisees that were observed even more strictly than the mandates of Scripture. Paul's use does not follow the Pharisees in promoting an extrabiblical set of instructions, but most assuredly does refer to specific instructions of belief and conduct. Church members who acted disorderly toward what he told them in person or wrote to them should feel the church's displeasure by its standing aloof from them.

Some instruction, or tradition, had to do with the necessity of disciplined, profitable work (2 Thess. 3:7–13). Other "tradition" had to do with the content of the gospel and was the truth which they had believed (2 Thess. 2:13) and the gospel through which they were called (2:14). These were the traditions they had been taught and in which they were to stand firm. If someone lived in conscious contradiction to these traditions (the inspired teachings of the apostle), the church must separate from him.

When Benjamin Keach discussed discipline, he treated three types of censure and restoration: private offenses, scandalous public behavior, and "Hereticks and Blasphemers." By heresy Keach meant any "perverse Opinion or Error in a fundamental Point of Religion." As examples he lists denying the "Being of God, or the Deity of Christ, or his Satisfaction, and Justification alone by his Righteousness, or to deny the Resurrection of the Body, or eternal Judgment, or the like."[16]

Keach rejected the argument that a person could not be condemned as a heretic if he held true to his own conscience. He felt sure that Hymenaeus and Alexander held their heresy with utmost confidence and were conscientiously committed to it. Nevertheless, they were delivered up to Satan—placed under church censure.[17]

The Philadelphia Association adopted precisely the same position with respect to a person's denying the "foreknowledge of God, concerning all future evil as well as good." After giving three reasons why such an opinion was a grievous error, they entertained the following query. "Whether a member of the church holding

110

such an opinion, endeavors to propagate it, and obstinately persists in it, is not worthy of the highest censure, notwithstanding he pleads matter of conscience?" The answer provided to the query is instructive: "We judge such worthy of the highest censure; because a church is to proceed against a person who is erroneous in judgment, as well as against one vicious in practice, notwithstanding they may plead conscience in the affair."[18] The Charleston Association, likewise, placed within discipline the task of having "the bitter roots of false doctrine eradicated."[19]

Richard Furman, in listing issues for which a church has a stewardship in enforcing the "laws of Christ," speaks of "the admission of persons to membership; watching over and admonishing those who are its members; and excluding such as become scandalously wicked and obstinately impenitent." That his is peculiarly a congregational matter Scripture enforces in showing Paul's treatment "on the subject of judging and excommunication as the proper work for the body of the church at Corinth; and in a similar manner does he address the Thessalonians, respecting their disorderly members."[20]

P. H. Mell (1814–1888) listed "open rebellion to the faith and practice of the church" as one type of public offense deserving of censure. Just as those who are weak in faith may be admitted as members, so those who are weak in faith do not incur censure for doctrinal immaturity and questions. The operative phrase for Mell was "open rebellion" as that for the Philadelphia Association referred to a person who held error tenaciously and "endeavors to propagate it, and obstinately persists in it." "Open rebellion" and obstinacy differ qualitatively from weakness, but sincerity, in the faith. Mell summarized the nature of a doctrinal offense in this way:

> Let not this citation, however, be misunderstood. No reference is made to those who are ignorant of Gospel doctrines, or who even have doubts as to the Scriptural character of those held by the Church. A gospel church is not a circle of doctrinal proficients, but a school for learners, where those who are acquainted only with the alphabet of the gospel—with the first principles of the doctrine of Christ—may receive instruction, and grow as they follow on to know the Lord. The only qualifications for admission into a gospel church is repentance towards God, and faith in the Lord Jesus Christ. There are doubtless, multitudes in the churches who know nothing of the profound doctrines of grace, or even have misgivings as to the correctness of the interpretations put

111

upon them, who are yet guilty of no offence, and members in good standing. Reference is had to those, solely, who declare open war against the doctrines and practices of the Church and engage in active efforts to subvert and destroy them. The Church is bound to hold these as "public offenders;" and if there is to be any difference in the treatment of their case and in that of other public offenders, it is to be found in the injunction, "A man that is a heretic, *after the first and second admonition reject.*" Tit. iii. 10.[21]

Perseverance in a lifestyle of carelessness and slothfulness also sets a foundation for discipline. From these spring other evils, according to the associational records of the west country in England in 1657. A time of grievous dryness and worldliness in the churches led to a strong, if not scathing, remonstrance against the coldness, pride, and lack of Christian compassion in the churches. Ministers were urged to "bear faithful testimony against every evil way that is hated and abhored [sic] of God." Even with this, the corresponding ministers knew all too well that many were "sermon-proof and epistle-proof," and so entrenched in their aloofness "that they have wrested all weapons out of the hands of saints and minister that have been formed against them." The time had come, according to the letter, to go beyond the "testimony of words" and "proceed to take some effectual course that sin or sinners may be purged out of the house of God."[22]

Conclusion

Maintaining faithfulness to the ideal of regenerate church membership enlists all the energies of a careful, sensitive, and doctrinally mature mind. It calls for the sort of person the writer of Hebrews desired to see:

Concerning him [Melchizedek] we have much to say, and it is hard to explain, since you have become dull of hearing. For though by this time you ought to be teachers, you have need again for someone to teach you the elementary principles of the oracles of God, and you have come to need milk and not solid food. For everyone who partakes only of milk is not accustomed to the word of righteousness, for he is an infant. But solid food is for the mature, who because of practice have their senses trained to discern good and evil. (Heb. 5:11–14)

That most distinctive feature of Baptist life, the doctrine of the church, will not survive in its historical form apart from comprehensive doctrinal reformation. A minimally doctrinal ecclesiology loses its meaning and cannot lay claim to that lofty biblical image and spiritual reality known as the body of Christ. Other Baptist issues related to church could be investigated, including the liberty of conscience, with a view to demonstrating their doctrinal foundations. But this must suffice to encourage an ongoing doctrinal recovery not only for the sake of the truth of those doctrines themselves but for the protection and purity of Christ's bride.

Chapter 10

Theology That Will
Support a Worldview

Let This Mind Be in You

Jesus Christ gave himself as an atonement to rescue his people from this present evil age (Gal. 1:4). So impregnated with the world system that every thought reflects the folly of arrogant but hopeless rebels, the newly transformed mind must undergo radical alteration. The washing of regeneration sovereignly effected by the Holy Spirit has replaced the old love of the world and slavery to sin with a love for God, his truth, his people, and slavery to righteousness. The Spirit, through the Word of God, reorders the Christian's mind so that his thoughts, and thus his life, reflect more and more the character of Christ (2 Cor. 3:12–18). This process may be called the development of a Christian worldview.

The Philosophical Task

The use of the phrase, "Christian worldview," most often refers to the development of a Christian critique of non-Christian philosophies. This is a very helpful practice. Unanswered philosophical challenges often lead to great distress for Christians confronted with alternative worldviews and can create severe ambivalence in Christian witness. E. Y. Mullins in his helpful work *Why Is Christianity True?* showed the weaknesses of several current philosophies and the relevant strengths of Christianity. He spoke of pantheism, materialism, agnosticism, and evolution, drawing an appropriate conclusion about the shortcomings of each worldview as compared to Christianity.

For example, Mullins closed the chapter on agnosticism by declaring, "its lack of moral force is a sufficient condemnation of agnosticism, to say nothing of its intellectual inconsistencies."[1] His work is succinct but insightful, concise but sufficient in scope. His conclusion about pantheism demonstrates these strengths.

> We now conclude: Pantheism fails, because it ignores so many facts of science and of human consciousness; because it forces a solution at points where the problem as yet seems insoluble; because while it moves far away from a fact basis for its theory it leaves us with as many unfathomable mysteries as ever; and because it is content with affirmations instead of demonstration. Thus at no point—science, philosophy, ethics or religion—is it a satisfactory explanation of the world.[2]

A twenty-first-century critique of non-Christian worldviews that includes a cogent presentation of a Christian worldview comes from the pen of L. Russ Bush, academic dean and professor of philosophy at Southeastern Baptist Theological Seminary. His argument for a Christian worldview is set in the context of a series of modern alternatives related to the idea of "advancement." In short, "advancement" means that the world is in process of developing, becoming supposedly better and better, and no present reality can be esteemed as absolute truth.

Bush traces the philosophical pedigree of advancement theory and concentrates primarily on naturalistic evolution as its most obvious manifestation. A number of theological and philosophical alternatives have emerged either as expressions of or reactions against the dehumanizing implications of naturalistic evolution. Bush shows how each of these shares the basic assumption of the concept of advancement. As a result, they also share its fallacies. As he summarizes the implications of his critique, he gives several principles by which worldviews may be evaluated.

> An alternative view is not proven worthy of acceptance merely by showing negative features of the dominant view, but valid criticism does provide some motivation for considering other possibilities.

115

The assumption that makes criticism possible is directly related to the relationship between truth and reality. The correct worldview is the one that does not contradict, misunderstand, or deny any part of reality. The comprehensiveness of worldviews is complete. Thus, the correctness of one excludes the possible correctness of another. The biblical God cannot both exist and not exist. The natural process cannot both be and not be the ultimate source of reality.

To prove one worldview false is not by itself enough to prove another one true, but it is a valuable preliminary step in such an argument. If a worldview can be shown to be internally contradictory and thus self-defeating, it is thereby shown to be false because the affirmation of a self-contradictory position is in itself a denial of that position.[3]

These classic philosophic approaches to the question of worldview have greatly encouraged many Christians and have helped them cope with the onslaught of unbelieving disdain for Christian truth. Such material must continue to have a place of high priority both in Christian churchmanship and theological education.

Transformed by the Renewing of Your Minds

I am speaking in this chapter, however, of another kind of worldview. Not only does Christian truth unfolded in biblical revelation challenge the philosophical assumptions that seek to minimize or eliminate the divine component of reality; it also challenges the innate, inbred, and culturally reinforced worldliness of our thoughts. In addition to the philosophical challenge Christians should learn to present to the prevailing intellectual culture, there must be an internal revolution in the way we view ourselves and our neighbors in light of biblical theology. We must learn to see Christian doctrine as so relevant and revitalizing that its implications redefine our entire being. A structural denominational change from moderates to inerrantists does not constitute a reformation without a corresponding revitalization of applied doctrine.

One key passage that shows the total revolution of perception of the world that the Christian must undergo is found in Romans 12:1–2. Paul contends there that the mercy of God as manifested in Christ's atoning work, the Spirit's work of transformation, the Father's sovereignty in the entire process of salvation ("by the mercies of God," a simplified summary of Paul's argument in Romans to this point) from eternal covenantal love ("whom He foreknew") to glorification ("He also glorified") calls for a lifestyle of worship ("spiritual service of worship") that involves the immolation of self ("present your bodies a living . . . sacrifice") in the interests of God-likeness ("holy . . . acceptable to God"). This is to be accomplished by a radical change in worldview. "Do not be conformed to this world, but be transformed by the renewing of your mind." This renewing of the mind provides the foundation for the testing and approving of the intrinsic goodness and perfection of God's will.

Church Credibility Requires It

Circular letters written from associations of Baptist churches to member churches in seventeenth-century England urged on all the members a serious and sober meditation on the transforming effect of doctrine. The meetings addressed several issues—some doctrinal point, judgments on practical issues and ecclesiological matters, and exhortations to holiness and transformation of life. These letters engaged both mind and affection to greater Christian consistency through showing the applicability of Christian doctrine.

Their historical context pressed on them the necessity of proving to be a peculiar people. They claimed to be a church of believers. The established church included everyone and brought pressure on Baptists to conform. Enemies brought many false accusations of immorality and unlawfulness and scrutinized their behavior for opportunities to attack. These pressures only made meticulous care on these issues ever-present in their Christian consciousness.

This concern may be seen clearly in the admonition written from the Midland Association to its member churches in October 1657. The letter expressed the desire "that you may adorn the pretious gospell of our Lord Jesus with a holy and humbell conversation and that you may presse forward towardes the marke that is sett before you and that you may be kept unblameable untill the coming of our Lord Jesus Christ."

They had prayed earnestly for the prosperity of "Zion in general" but more particularly "that wee might be thereby the more enabled to glorifie him in our generation and perform the duties of our relation each to other as becometh a people redeemed by Christ." They especially noted the necessity to "be more in consideration of those blessed cautions that our Lord hath left uppon record for to warne us that so a slugish and drowsie frame of spirit sease [seize] not uppon us."[4]

The "blessed cautions" included direct warning against worldliness and slug-gishness in spiritual matters, enforcing the point by reminding them of who they were by God's grace in this world. What implications did the doctrines of the gospel have for them as a people who were in the world but not of the world? Failure to take to heart the truths of their calling by the gospel had allowed the "world as a canker to eat out your affections to the Lord Jesus." Too often had they been "asleep in the lap of this Dalilah" so that their "locks have been cut off and you are but as other men." Worldly approval in some cases had "made the world too beautiful" in that Satan "hath shewed them the kingdomes of the earth and this hath bewitched them." This condition had made the families of Christians "so dry, useless, and unprofitable" and had eaten out all the "divine sweetness of regenerating and sanctifying grace."[5]

When the yearly reports of churches indicated no improvement, but only a pattern of "all the same things that wee have endeavored reformation of," the leaders seemed distressed. Church and family neglect, deadness and coldness still abounded in the churches. Apparently the churches were content merely to com-plain, to confess fault and sin without forsaking them. Only a true grasp of God's grace toward them could prompt humility and heavenly mindedness. The remedy for such sullen spirituality lay not in reprimand or moral exhortation, but in a mind absorbed by the kindness of God.

> Though wee find much cause of filling our luynes [lines] with com-plaints yet wee would not forget the kindnesse of the Lord both to you and us. And, first, that hee should make choyce of such unworthy ones and give his Sonne to dye for us and send forth his Spirrite in the Gospell of peace to call us from darkness. Yea when wee were running to the pit of missery to bring us backe and put us among his children, setting us together in the hevenly places in Christ Jesus, giving us the everlasting hope of everlasting glory. Yea, such things that eye hath not seene nor eare heard not entered into the heart of man so wee may cry out with David, Oh, how great is thy goodness which thou hast laid up for them that feare thee. May not our hearts leape for joye in the thoughts of this glory and bee much to the admiring the distinguishing grace of God that wee shaould [sic] be chosen, otheres left. We have also cause to take notice of the love of God and his power in keeping us to beare his name and owne his trueth where so many are lost in the dark above and many turned from the precious wayes of God.[6]

118

Holiness should pave the way for evangelism. The letter expressed deep gratitude that he had given "suckcesses in that great worke of conversion" by opening many "dores in severall parts for the teaching of the Gospell to the world." In light of such blessing, the churches must resolve that "henceforth yee walke not as the gentiles walked in the vanity of their wishes but that wee put off the old man which is corrupt and that wee put on the new man which after God is created in righteousnesse and true holinesse."

In addition to holiness of life, church order and church officers according to biblical example prepared the churches for evangelistic engagement. Those near at hand were of immediate concern—that is, "poor friendes lying in their blood (among whom you were in tymes past) may bee much upon your hearts before the Lord and that, both at home and abroad, you may much endeavor their conversion." Further afield, evangelism was encouraged: "And it may bee a very acceptable service to the Lord if you may bee sending forth the joyfull sound into darke partes remote from you."

Their view of life, in other words, must conform to doctrinal truth if they were to find spiritual joy, bear spiritual fruit, and propagate the Christian message. The biblical pattern for Christian living develops out of the radical changes implied in regeneration, forgiveness, justification, reconciliation, and the nature and attributes of God. A Christian worldview involves life transformation in light of doctrinal truth as well as intellectual engagement with prevailing philosophies and value systems. It involves correcting our own sinful actions and reactions in the world as well as refuting secularistic, naturalistic, materialistic, rationalistic, modernistic, or postmodernistic approaches to the world.

The Consistent Biblical Pattern

This is exactly what Paul had in mind when he spoke of "taking every thought captive to the obedience of Christ" (2 Cor. 10:5). Though it may be applied to the legitimacy of philosophical confrontation, its main emphasis concerns the relation between orthodox theology and holy living. The challenge to Paul's apostolic authority had grown severe and the misrepresentations of his character, his qualifications as an apostle, and his manner of conduct toward the Corinthians seemed to be taking root in their minds. In light of that, false apostles had been altering his gospel message and diminishing the person and work of Christ (11:3–4, 13–15). Paul's defense of his apostleship, including his gifts of power, his sufferings, and his motives, grew strong so they would not forsake either the

Christ or the gospel that he preached. He wanted to build them up, not destroy them (10:8; 12:19; 13:10). When he finally came to them, would he find them in the faith, or out of it? If they accepted false doctrine, they also would lead destructive lives.

> For I am afraid that perhaps when I come I may find you to be not what I wish and may be found by you to be not what you wish; that perhaps there may be strife, jealousy, angry tempers, disputes, slanders, gossip, arrogance, disturbances; I am afraid that when I come again my God may humiliate me before you, and I may mourn over many of those who have sinned in the past and not repented of the impurity, immorality and sensuality which they have practiced. (12:20–21)

A false theology leads directly to an untransformed life. A false gospel and a false Christ cannot lead to a rationale for holy living. On the other hand, when every speculation and every lofty thing "raised up against the knowledge of God" (2 Cor. 10:5) is brought into captivity to Christ, then a people will cleanse themselves "from all defilement of flesh and spirit, perfecting holiness in the fear of God" (2 Cor. 7:1).

Paul taught the Colossians how to develop transformed relationships through serious engagement with the truths of the divine nature and Christ's redemptive work. In chapter 3, Paul reminded the believers that they had an entirely new life, the prototype of which was already in heaven in Christ's glorified humanity (Col. 3:1–4). Since our present true life is in heaven and we actually will be glorified in the future, all that belongs to the life of rebellion and provokes divine wrath must be put to death. The members of this present body may already begin to reflect that glory that currently shines in Christ. The old self dominated by the depraved worldview gives way to the new self in the incipient stages of restoring the divine image (Col. 3:5–11). This is the worldview change Paul was looking for when he said, "I say this so that no one will delude you with persuasive argument" (Col. 2:4).

Each aspect of God's gracious dealing with his people has its own appropriate corollary in human conduct and attitude (Col. 3:12–17). "Therefore, God's chosen ones, holy and loved, put on heartfelt compassion, kindness, humility, gentleness, and patience" (Col. 3:12 HCSB). God's choice, his determination to set apart certain sinners (holy) to receive his redemptive love (loved) resulting in his patience with them should radically impact the way we respond personally. If we have been loved while godless, then we must be compassionate. We can never go beyond the compassion shown us by God.

We must also emulate the kindness of God, for when we were hated and hateful, he showed kindness in sending Jesus:

> For we too were once foolish, disobedient, deceived, captives of various passions and pleasures, living in malice and envy, hateful, detesting one another. But when the goodness and love for man appeared from God our Savior, He saved us . . . according to His mercy. (Titus 3:3–5 HCSB)

Election shows us that we have nothing of our own about which to boast, but we owe all to God's sovereign choice; humility, therefore, is the only appropriate response. Election also has established a component of gentleness and patience in God's dealing with us. Although he could have destroyed us in eternal wrath and kept us under miserable temporal judgments until that destruction, he has been filled with gentleness and his patience has extended to infinite lengths. Paul had experienced this (1 Tim. 1:16). Therefore, to change the personal worldview of his readers, he reminded them that they should see themselves as well as other people through the lens of election.

C. D. Mallary (1801–1864) argued for the sanctifying influences of a healthy reflection on the issue that "guilty, hell-deserving sinners are absolutely dependent on His unmerited favor for pardon and salvation." He is not moved at all by human will but by "His own free, sovereign, gracious pleasure" and bestowed through Christ "according to His stable and everlasting purposes." These doctrines are to be studied "with a view to holy practical ends." When that is done, it will "secure to the soul a precious, fragrant, ripening holiness" in a context that "will smite down their pride and fill them with adoring wonder."[7]

Forgiveness by the blood of Christ also has a powerful effect in changing our understanding of the world. By the sacrifice of his only begotten, well-beloved Son, God has opened the door of forgiveness for sinners. We have been forgiven at infinite cost, and have been lovingly welcomed to benefit from what Christ has done. Remember, Christ died for the helpless and the ungodly (Rom. 5:6). If we absorb that reality into the way we perceive relationships, how can we ever be reserved about forgiveness? What can be done to us that has not been done sevenfold by us against God?

How would this transform marriage and the willingness to forgive if we consistently acted in accordance with the truth of our forgiveness? Christ emptied himself of heavenly glory and put our well-being, our best interest, before his own immutable pleasure, and submitted himself to the vagaries of human suffering and fickle relationships (Phil. 2:7–8; Rom. 15:3). No human agent ever gave him any comfort or encouragement as he undertook the most extreme act of love ever performed.

If both wife and husband lived with that theological reality well entrenched in their hearts and approached marriage with deep gratitude for such infinite mercy shown them, the tension and argumentation that arises from taking personal offense would diminish greatly. We would discover much less pride to offend and far fewer rights to maintain. When we consider others better than ourselves and their interests more pressing (Phil. 2:3–4), we are much slower to be defensive toward them or feel it our right to confront them.

In social relationships the same theological model operates. "Let every one of us please his neighbour for his good to edification," Paul wrote (Rom. 15:2 KJV). The reason is centered on the incarnation and atonement: "For even Christ pleased not himself; but, as it is written, The reproaches of them that reproached thee fell on me" (Rom. 15:3 KJV).

The reality of our helplessness (Rom. 5:6) throughout this transaction should transform our attitudes toward providing help for the helpless. Those who have no ability to respond to our kindness, who cannot reciprocate either with action, or money, or emotional acknowledgement must nevertheless receive our care. Those actions that most closely reflect the redemptive mercies of God are often the things that are never seen and yet involve the most arduous and thankless labor. Those tasks that have the greatest tendency to sanctify and show that the heart is being fit for heaven are those things that are the most menial and least celebrated and desired among men (Mark 9:31–37; 10:42–45). That the Son of Man came not to be served but to serve and give his life a ransom, if grasped mind and soul, would create a true servant spirit and evoke servant action on the part of Christians. This involves a true alteration of worldview.

A healthy doctrine of the Trinity does wonders for a person's personal worldview. After all, the Trinity is the fountain and foundation of all reality. The triune God has created the world to reflect his nature. When we contemplate the nature of the Trinity, therefore, and take to heart the attribute that gives the one God an eternal three-personed existence, we create a fabric from which unity may function in the midst of diversity. For this reason, Paul wrote, "And above all these put on love, which binds everything together in perfect harmony" (Col. 3:14 RSV).

The biblical teaching of the Trinity shows three infinitely excellent persons all having the same essential deity, yet having distinctive and person-appropriate modes of relating, both within the eternal divine essence and to the universe in creation, providence, and redemption. If love is the eternal fountain of the three-personed God, then love is the key to unity in the world he has created, particularly in the church for which Jesus died in obedience to the will of the Father. Nothing could be more wholesome for church unity, sympathetic relationships, and wholesome fellowship than the profound wonder and heartfelt joy in the doctrine of the Trinity.

In a fallen world, however, the road to unity and love involves a radical restoration of relationship. Christ's reconciling work has produced peace between God and sinners. For this reason Paul can say, "Let the peace of Christ rule in your hearts, to which indeed you were called in one body" (3:15). If God has taken the initiative and removed the offense he had against us, such a reconciling work should affect our desire for peace with others. We were at enmity with God, and he also justly stood as our enemy because of our unjust aggression against his lawful rule. He has taken action to appease his wrath and restore our hearts to that proper subjection to him, and he gives the call, "Be reconciled to God." On this basis he has preached peace to sinners in all places. Since the eternal God has pursued the making of peace as a priority in the manifestation of his glory, we should let Christ's peace rule in our hearts.

An understanding of reconciliation by Christ's death, including the destruction of the barrier between Jew and Gentile (Eph. 2:14) and the absolute claim that Christ's death gives him over our lives (2 Cor. 5:15), should motivate us to refuse to nurse any offense. Grudges have no place in the interpersonal relationships of Christians. To allow personal offense, hurt feelings, or a social *faux pas* to bring division in a local church contradicts the act by which the church was established. A part of the renewing of the mind, the alteration of personal worldview, hinges on a personal processing of Christ's work of reconciliation.

Finally, Paul admonished the Colossians to let the "word of Christ dwell in you richly in all wisdom; teaching and admonishing one another" (Col. 3:16 KJV). The word of God must prevail; its rule, moreover, comes through a thorough understanding and full appropriation in application. When the word dwells in us richly, we have absorbed its content, understood the leading themes of it, their relationship to each other, and the power of their truth. Systematic theology, or confessions of faith, no longer impress us as unrealistic, academic barriers to the dynamic life of Scripture but as friends to give guidance in a rich journey through the Word.

Knowing this Word as the "word of Christ" shows that we see its expression most accurately when we are able to relate it to Christ. We are driven not by mere arbitrary and undisciplined sentiment but by awareness of the divine intent to restore God's people and display his glory through the covenantal arrangements with the well-beloved Son of God. All the contents of the Bible point us in some way to Christ. Jesus' religious opponents showed their ignorance of the Word of God, when their knowledge of it did not lead them to him.

"And the Father who sent me has himself borne witness about me" (John 5:37 ESV), Jesus told them, in a clear reference to the Father's intention that the Old Testament Scriptures should lead its readers to recognize and embrace the Messiah. Jesus continued, "His voice you have never heard, his form you have never seen; and you do not have his word abiding in you, for you do not believe him whom he has sent" (v. 37b RSV). To summarize his judgment of the source of their resistance he said, "You search the scriptures, because you think that in them you have eternal life; and it is they that bear witness to me; yet you refuse to come to me that you may have life" (vv. 39–40 RSV).

Not only to his detractors did Jesus emphasize the Christocentric nature of Scripture, but he showed the same thing to his disciples that their faith would be strong, informed, and formidable. He told those two bewildered and distressed disciples as he joined them on the road to Emmaus, "O foolish men, and slow of heart to believe all that the prophets have spoken!" (Luke 24:25 RSV). Had they seen the entire message of the Old Testament, how all its history, all its poetry, all its wisdom and all its prophecy pointed to him, they would have known that it was "necessary that the Christ should suffer these things and enter into his glory" (v. 26). To put them on the road to a mature, cross-carrying faith, therefore, he began "with Moses and all the prophets, he interpreted to them in all the scriptures the things concerning himself" (v. 27).

Our understanding of Scripture will be focused correctly and bear vibrant and lasting fruit when it is handled as the word of Christ. Our worldview will be transformed when we relate all our activities ("whatever you do in word or deed") to the "name of the Lord Jesus" and live in gratitude that our approach to the Father comes "through Him" (Col. 3:17).

When we admonish one another in wisdom, we encourage our sisters and brothers to act in a way consistent with the truth of Scripture. We do not desire a spirituality, that is, transformation of personal worldview, that rises above doctrine. In fact, we must pursue lives that more and more approximate the beautiful lineaments of clearly articulated, Christian doctrine. We desire that the rich truths of Scripture, expressed as discreet yet indivisibly related doctrines, so saturate our minds and affections that our conduct will be a reflection of the gospel and its truth.

We will know that justification is more than just a doctrine; it transforms our hearts to relationships saturated with grace. We will know that election is more than just an objective description of how God goes after a people for himself; it commends to us a life of patience and kindness and active pursuit of friendship to do good to others. When we encourage others with the blessed and infinitely glorious truth of the Trinity, we purify our worship of him and set forth a goal for unity through the binding sinews of love. When we admonish one another in the wisdom of reconciliation, we hold out hope that all barriers can be overcome through just, loving, and holy strategy under the blessing of God's grace.

Our personal worldview can be radically altered through eternal truth; we can approve the things that are excellent in order to be found "sincere and blameless until the day of Christ" (Phil. 1:10).

C. D. Mallary, who treated the entire spectrum of biblical doctrine in its tendency to produce holiness, summarized the power of biblical realities in promoting personal piety and reformation in a section on "active faith."

> At first the sinner, convinced of sin, renouncing all the works of righteousness which he has done, and all other human dependencies, flies to Christ for refuge and complacently relies on Him as his wisdom, righteousness, sanctification, and redemption. He is now accepted, pardoned, and justified; he is united to the Savior by faith; he is now a child of God by faith in Christ Jesus. But that faith which first bears the soul to Christ abides in the bosom, a permanent and living principle, depending upon Him at all times, and trusting Him through life for all needed good. And, moreover, that faith which rests on the Savior secures in the bosom a cordial reception of all God's testimony, as far as the mind progresses in the right understanding of the terms in which it is propounded. It takes God at His word in all things. It expands and ripens into the sweet revealed truth at large; the truth that concerns ourselves, the Father, The Savior, the Holy Spirit; the works, providence, and government of God; the soul, the Church, angels, eternity.

To faith is assigned, by the Scriptures of truth, a most dignified position, it has much, very much, to do in the whole spiritual history of the saint; and according as it prospers or declines does the soul prosper or decline in its vital interests. Without it, it is impossible to enjoy God, to obey God, to please God. It nurtures the comfort, quietude, and stability of the soul. By faith we stand; by faith we walk; by faith we live, labor, fight, and conquer. It is that by which we purify our hearts; it is the victory that overcomes the world, the shield by which we quench the fiery darts of the wicked. It gives boldness and success in prayer, a sweet odor to praise, a spiritual excellence to our patient enduring. What is the word read, or heard, or remembered, unmixed with faith? A profitless thing. Faith, by receiving the word of God in its true import and for its true intent, converts it into precious nourishment for the soul; feeding by faith upon the manna of truth, the soul is made prosperous—it flourishes in beauty and in strength, in hope and in gladness.[8]

This sort of worldview not only will be the most unanswerable challenge to the unbelieving philosophies of the world, but it will be the true fruit of ongoing reformation in the churches. We must strive always to have a holy discontent with our present status that it not be *quo* but pursue the status of *ecclesia reformata, semper reformanda*—a church that is reformed and always reforming.

Epilogue

When one reviews Scripture to discern evidences of a real working of God's Spirit among men, one issue in particular presses to the front: the Word of God is given prominence. This occurred in the Protestant Reformation of the sixteenth century. From Germany under Luther, to Switzerland under Zwingli, to Geneva under Calvin, to the Anabaptists spread abroad, to England under Cranmer, to Scotland under Knox, Scripture began its reign as the sole authority in discerning God's Word to man. This led to redefining the importance of the early councils and creeds, to an investigation of sound principles of biblical interpretation, to serious study of Greek and Hebrew, to critical examination of the variety of biblical texts available, to a rejection of the authority of the pope and his tradition.

The Reformation did not terminate with the initial generation, but it set in motion a lengthy investigation of doctrine and ecclesiology. This established unity and clarity of doctrine within large groups but also division and vigorous doctrinal disagreement in other spheres. The goal of all groups, however, was to submit to the clear teaching of Scripture. Southern Baptists have taken that first step with good evidence that God is at work. Stewardship of this recovery calls for long-term evaluation and renewal.

One stage of development in the Reformation focused on the development of creeds and confessions of faith. The 95 Theses of Luther led to more detailed statements of faith on a broader spectrum of subjects. These affirmed what Lutherans held in common with all Christians, their peculiar points of distinction, and the articles within Catholicism that they rejected. The Augsburg Confession set the standard for Lutheran doctrine. That statement plus a series of others which settled a variety of Lutheran controversies eventually were gathered together in the Book of Concord.

Similarly, statements of faith written by Calvin for Geneva, the Belgic Confession by Guido de Bres, the Heidelberg Catechism by Zacharius Ursinus, the Second Helvetic Confession, the Canons of the Synod of Dort, and the Westminster Confession of Faith form a formidable body of theological literature that define Reformed Christianity. The confessions were not viewed as rivals to biblical authority or superior to it or even authoritative *per se*. They were seen as guides to understanding Scripture, witnesses to its clarity, and increasingly incisive and faithful presentations of biblical truth. They clearly presented the positive affirmations of the Reformed faith while they denied doctrines of other groups that they considered as unfaithful to, or even destructive of, biblical truth.

Baptists, keeping faith with the spirit of the Reformation of which they were a part, wrote their own confessions, largely within this Reformed stream of thought. In these they agreed with the large body of other Reformation Christians. Other issues, particularly the doctrine of the church, they articulated differently, but, in their opinion, more biblically and more consistently with the Reformation understanding of salvation by grace through faith.

This difference points out that ecclesiology went through a separate development during the Reformation and led to even more divisions than other doctrinal issues. While the Puritans worked for a more pure and thorough reformation within the Church of England, and the Separatists found that effort to be vain, both groups retained infant baptism and argued that it was the duty of the government to repress false religion and use its power to enforce true religion.

Baptists considered themselves thorough reformers in that issue. Baptists, while considering themselves in harmony with many Puritan ideals of church purity and discipline, believed the only way to attain that goal was through fostering a church composed of born-again people only. They found many good biblical reasons for this conviction and also argued that their view most clearly fulfilled the ideal of a church composed of visible saints only. Their views of discipline, their argument for separation of church and state, their pursuit of liberty of conscience—all these flow from this theological commitment of regeneration preceding church membership.

All the Reformers—Luther, Zwingli, Bullinger, Calvin, Cranmer, Hubmaier, Knox, and especially the Puritans—believed that Reformation should encourage holiness and intensify nonsuperstitious devotion to God. The transformation of life, that a person might be thoroughly given to the glory of God, was the ultimate goal of pure doctrine. Reformation without a sanctifying power on church members is no reformation.

A true reformation, therefore, goes through many stages and investigates the full range of biblical truth. It gives rise to confessions, discussions of ecclesiology, and the investigation of cases of conscience for the sake of godly living. If this resurgence of conservatism in Southern Baptist life is a reformation, all these issues will be taken seriously.

There is no need, however, to reinvent the wheel. This reformation has begun with a great historical advantage. Southern Baptists have arrested the decline from biblical authority and have restated their own historic commitment to biblical infallibility while resisting the many historically conditioned and highly nuanced attempts to undermine it. A large part of the formal principle of the Protestant and Baptist view of authority is well in place.

In addition, the Baptist confessional tradition stands as a noble witness to an active and theologically aware heritage. Activities leading to the revision of the *Baptist Faith and Message* that culminated with its adoption in 2000 show that a serious engagement with that heritage has arisen in some places. This should encourage us. Hopefully, the importance and benefits of a thorough knowledge of the heads of doctrine in the various Baptist confessions can be more deeply enmeshed in the worship and study of local churches. Mental courage in church life will promote a desire to leave no doctrine behind. "We must not be afraid to learn and to avow what God is not afraid to teach," Mallary reminds us.[1] Reformation will be stillborn without increasing doctrinal zeal for the full platform of God's truth.

Ecclesiology brings the whole spectrum of Protestant doctrine together in a distinctive way for Baptists. Our commitment to regenerate church membership, and thus credobaptism (baptism of believers only), hinges on the conscientious application of several serious practical issues. The theory and content of preaching, the practice of evangelism, and the growth and maintenance of the church—all these are inherently connected with the issue of church membership. A serious look at our church membership and attendance statistics will tell a frightening story. Its theological implications have a seriousness and complexity that challenge the quest for reformation. The good beginning can come to a stumbling halt if we refuse to grant serious theological reflection and faithful remedies to a problem caused by years of carelessness.[2]

Spirituality as expressed in many circles often is seen as an experience of encounter that transcends doctrine. Doctrine, in fact, often appears to be something of a hindrance to meaningful experience. Such experientialism is a fast road to decline and apostasy. It is true that bare doctrine unconnected to the heart blows a cold wind on spiritual growth. At the same time, no spiritual growth or experiential fire can be true and transformative if it is not knowledgeably connected with some genuine aspect of revealed biblical truth. Reformation must recapture the authentic characteristics of true spirituality.

The present challenge, therefore, is self-judgment. It is time to give attention to problems that continue to present a serious challenge to Baptist viability. While vigilance must endure in every area that was threatened by the insidious impact of the moderate contingency, many difficulties confront the church that have little or nothing to do with that influence. It has everything to do with personal carelessness, impatience, and loss of doctrinal nerve. Motivation for ministerial success comes often from surveys that determine pragmatically what is working; these observations then transfer into church theory. Though lip service is given to biblical authority, that which seems most dominant is the simple observation of success in terms of the immediate gratification of visible increase.

This practical pragmatism leads soon to theological minimalism. The theological problem is less obvious because it does not take the form of an ideological attack on biblical authority or historically received Baptist doctrine. The part of reformation that identified and gradually eliminated, mostly by attrition and resignation, the detractors from biblical inerrancy was easy compared to the next part. Can conservatives judge themselves? Can conservatives admit mistakes, long-term mistakes, and undertake serious reformation of their own destructive tendencies? Can we join Pogo and Albert and say, "We have found the enemy, and he is us?"

An external contest with forces hostile to recovery can soon become an internal test of purity of heart and genuine clarity of theological vision. The danger of forfeiting what has been gained always looms large. We must not substitute ignoring biblical authority for denying biblical authority. We must not substitute fanaticism for agnosticism. We must not substitute a sliced-and-diced and amputated gospel for the inclusivist perversions of the past.

It is only appropriate that we let Martin Luther have the last word. He saw how quickly Reformation can give way to compromise and infidelity. Luther warned that the pope's antigospel contrivances were replaced by newer but nonetheless dangerous methods of hiding the offense of the gospel. Observe carefully the dynamic described by Luther.

First he noted that some people already had arisen in Protestant churches who found the free grace of the gospel an offense. The pope and his devotees, who claimed the exclusive right of being called Christian, should have been grateful for a recovery of the true gospel but only set themselves to oppose and persecute it. Many who benefited greatly by the recovery of true doctrine and rejoiced in release from the oppressive man-made religion of Roman Catholicism soon lost interest in pursuing that purity with sincerity and vigor. Again they forgot the power of the grace of God and the freedom that it gives and even came to despise it. They substituted fanaticism or religious fervor without a true doctrinal support and false teaching, doctrines that altered or repressed the sharp edges of the free grace of God. May we be warned.

> But now the dear, blessed time has come, and there is a change, I say, so that people live and appear who wish neither to see nor to hear, neither to know nor to tolerate this rich grace and this highest favor of God bestowed gratuitously.
>
> Just as we also at present and easily understand now those who wish to be the Church and to be called Christians, the Pope and bishops with their followers, who should lift their hands to heaven and thank God for their deliverance from darkness and blindness that they have again the pure light of the Gospel; these bring fire and water, wet their sword and polish their weapons to exterminate from the earth those who teach and confess the pure Gospel, and there are so many unthankful, false Christians among us just like them, who despise this salvation in the most defiant manner. Formerly, when we were captives under the Pope's tyranny, burdened with the preaching of lies, relating to the indulgences, purgatory and all the dreams of the monks, what a sighing and longing there was then in all the world for the true preaching of the Gospel. How gladly would one then have given, labored and suffered all things possible to secure true instruction and comfort, and to be delivered with a good conscience from the fearful martyrdom of the confessional and other oppressive burdens imposed by the Pope! And how happy were many pious people at first because of this deliverance who learned it and thanked God for it! But now, how many are there who rejoice from their hearts and acknowledge how blessed they are in that they can see and hear this? How soon they took offense at this blessed treasure and then sought something else, when they forgot all they had received, and the world became again filled with fanaticism and false teachings.[3]

Endnotes

Introduction

1. Jerry Sutton, *The Baptist Reformation, The Conservative Resurgence in the Southern Baptist Convention* (Nashville: Broadman & Holman, 2000).

2. Ibid., 475–85.

3. For example, see Barry Hankins, *Uneasy in Babylon* (Tuscaloosa: University of Alabama Press, 2002); Russell H. Dilday, *Columns: Glimpses of a Seminary under Assault* (Macon, Ga.: Smyth & Helwys, 2004).

Chapter 1

1. Paige Patterson, *Strange Fire in the Holy of Holies* (Dallas: Criswell Center for Biblical Studies, 1980), 15. This was the third and final publication of the Shophar Papers. It was built on the death of Nadab and Abihu recorded in Leviticus 10:1–2, plus the instructions for sacrifice in Exodus 30:1–10 and Leviticus 16:11–13. Patterson concluded that denominational leadership tended to absolutize their positions and programs and judge the denominational viability of churches on the basis of their consent to these man-made programs. They were substituting the "strange fire" of denominational programs for the biblically warranted autonomy of the local congregation.

2. Ibid., 23.

3. Fisher Humphreys, *The Way We Were,* rev. ed. (Macon Ga.: Smyth & Helwys, 2002). Humphreys argues that many doctrinal aspects of a minority position among Baptists now are being incorporated into Southern Baptist life and will alter it for the worse.

Chapter 2

1. John Smyth, *The Works of John Smyth*, ed. W. T. Whitley, 2 vols. (Cambridge: At the University Press, 1915), 2:752–53.

2. Andrew Fuller, "Creeds and Subscriptions," in *The Complete Works of the Rev. Andrew Fuller*, 3:451.

3. Ibid., 449.

4. Ibid.

5. Ibid.

6. Smyth, 2:752.

7. Joseph Ivimey, *History of the English Baptists*, 4 vols. (London, 1811–30), 4:366.

8. B. A. Copass to E. Y. Mullins (12 January 1900) in Mullins letter file in archives, Boyce Memorial Library, The Southern Baptist Theological Seminary.

9. Abraham Booth, *A Confession of Faith Delivered at His Ordination* (n.p.: [1769]), 24.

10. Charles Deweese, "Theological Variety: Should We Celebrate It or Curse It?"

11. Roger Olson, *The Mosaic of Christian Belief* (Downers Grove: InterVarsity Press, 2002), 26. Olson is arguing for serious theological reflection that avoids both a formless, nondoctrinal "folk religion" as well as "the specter of inquisitions."

12. William Stokes, "Essay on Creeds" in *The History of the Midland Association of Baptist Churches from Its Rise in the Year 1655 to 1855* (London: H. Theobald, 1855), 10–11, 13.

13. Ibid., 15.

14. Ibid., 15–16.

15. Editor, "An Explanation of the Use of Creeds among Baptists," in *Western Baptist Review*, vol. 1, no. 3 (November 1845), 140–41.

16. S. M. Noel, "Circular Letter," in *Minutes of the Franklin Association of Baptists* (Bloomfield, Ky.: W. H. Holmes, 1826), 6.

17. Ibid., 7.

18. Ibid., 9. Noel acknowledges his indebtedness to Samuel Miller's treatment of creeds for the shape of his argument in some sections of the circular letter.

19. G. D. B. Pepper, "Doctrinal History and Position," in *Baptists and the National Centenary*, ed. Lemuel Moss (Philadelphia: American Baptist Publication Society, 1876), reprinted as a separate pamphlet (Lewisburg, Pa.: Heritage Publishers, 1976), 10.

20. Ibid., 11.

21. Ibid., 12.

22. Ibid., 15.

23. Francis Wayland, *The Principles and Practices of Baptist Churches,* ed. John Howard Hinton (London: J. Heaton & Son, 1861), 1.

24. Ibid., 3.

25. Ibid., 2.

26. Ibid., 4–7.

27. Ibid., 4.

28. J. P. Boyce, "Three Changes in Theological Institutions," in *James Petigru Boyce: Selected Writings,* ed. Timothy George (Nashville: Broadman Press, 1989), 52.

29. B. H. Carroll, "Colossians, Ephesians, and Hebrews," in *An Interpretation of the English Bible,* ed. J. B. Cranfill (Grand Rapids: Baker Book House, 1973 reprint of Nashville: Broadman Press, 1948), 149.

30. J. B. Gambrell, "Concerning the Uses of Creedal Statements," *Baptist Standard,* 22 January 1914, 1.

31. Carroll, "Colossians, Ephesians, and Hebrews, 140, 145–46.

Chapter 3

1. Robert Hall Jr., *The Works of Robert Hall, A. M.,* 6 vols. (London: Holdsworth and Ball, 1833), 1:256–57.

2. Basil Manly Jr., "The Wisdom of Winning Souls," in *The Baptist Preacher* (November 1854), 190–91.

3. Ibid., 192.

4. Craig Bird, "Preaching in the 21st Century" in *Western Recorder* (23 November 2004), 1.

5. Ibid., quoting Julie Pennington-Russell, pastor of Calvary Baptist Church, Waco, Texas.

6. Robert Hall Jr., *Works,* 1:251–52.

7. Ibid., 1:250.

8. John A Broadus, *A Treatise on the Preparation and Delivery of Sermons,* rev. (1898) by Edwin Charles Dargan. Forty-second edition with preface by A. T. Robertson and revised bibliography by C. S. Gardner (New York: George H. Doran Company, 1926), 243–44.

9. Charles Spurgeon, *Lectures to My Students,* Second Series (London: Passmore & Alabaster, 1881), 184.

10. Spurgeon, *Lectures,* 180.

Chapter 4

1. Hanserd Knollys, *Christ Exalted: A Lost Sinner Sought, and Saved by Christ* (London: Jane Coe, 1645), 27.

2. John Brine, *A Refutation of Arminian Principles* (London: Printed and sold by A. Ward, 1743), 10–11.

3. Andrew Fuller, *The Life and Death of Rev. Andrew Fuller,* ed. John Ryland (London: Button & Son, 1816), 153–54.

4. Ibid., in article XII and XV of Fuller's personal confession of faith, 105–106.

5. Andrew Broaddus, *The Sermons and Other Writings of the Rev. Andrew Broaddus with a Memoir of His Life by J. B. Jeter,* ed. Andrew Broaddus, son of the author (New York: Lewis Colby, 1852), 119–20.

6. Fuller wrote a memoir of Pearce at his death. Andrew Fuller, "Memoirs of the Rev. Samuel Pearce, M.S." in *The Complete Works of the Rev. Andrew Fuller,* 3 vols. (Harrisonburg, Va.: Sprinkle Publications, 1988), 3:367–446.

7. Ibid., 3:389.

8. Ibid., 3:391.

9. *The History of the Midland Association of Baptist Churches* (London: R. Theobald; Birmingham: John W. Showell, 1855), 115.

10. Samuel Pearce, "Circular Letter, 1794," in *The History of the Midland Association of Baptist Churches,* 115–21.

11. *Works of Fuller,* 3:434.

12. Ibid., 3:435.

13. Ibid., 3:438.

14. Ibid., 3:439.

15. *The Complete Works of the Rev. Andrew Fuller,* 3:345–51, in a sermon entitled, "The Pastor's Address to His Christian Hearers, Entreating Their Assistance in Promoting the Interest of Christ." Fuller solicits the aid of church members in ministry to "serious and humble Christians," by praying for the minister in his public duty of preaching and by opening their minds to him concerning the effect that the preaching has. They must also be concerned with those who are "disorderly walkers" by joining lovingly and impartially the task of admonition and exhortation of fellow Christians. Hopefully, by this practice some cases of discipline might be avoided, but if necessary they must join with the leaders in the discipline of those who continue to walk in a disorderly manner. Third, they should be sensitive about how to deal with those who are "inquiring after the way of salvation." Fourth, they should cultivate means by which they can introduce and recommend the gospel to neighbors and townspeople who live in a "state of unconcernedness about salvation." Finally, they should live in a way that would enable ministers to use strong language about the "holy and happy effects" of the gospel.

16. Ibid., 3:349.

17. Ibid., 3:350.

18. Ibid.

19. Robert Sandeman was a theologian in Scotland whom Fuller worked with

amicably in the early stages of making collections for the support of the work of the Missionary Society. Eventually, however, he had to oppose Sandeman's theology just as strongly as he opposed hyper-Calvinism. Sandeman believed that sinners confronted with the gospel did not need any special operation of the Holy Spirit to enable saving faith. Fuller argued that the new birth must precede repentance and faith to establish a moral texture and disposition in the soul conducive to a loathing of sin and desire for righteousness.

Chapter 5

1. W. F. Broaddus, Centennial Sermon of the Potomac Baptist Association of Virginia (Published by the Acting Board, 1867), 20–21. This pagination is from a handwritten copy of the sermon.

2. David Benedict, *A General History of the Baptist Denomination in America and Other Parts of the World*, 2 vols. (Boston: Lincoln & Edmands, 1813; reprint, Freeport, N.Y.: Books for Libraries Press, 1971), 2:109–10.

3. William Fristoe, *A Concise History of the Ketocton Baptist Association* (Staunton: Printed by William Gilman Lyford, 1808), 41–42.

4. Ibid., 47.

5. Manly in a letter to his wife, 4 September 1846.

6. George Boardman Taylor ("G. B. T.") in *The Religious Herald* about June 1861.

7. The following discussion and quotes come from J. B. Jeter in a series of articles on "Protracted Meetings" in the *Religious Herald* (8 March, 15 March, 22 March, 29 March, 5 April, 1866).

8. William E. Hatcher, "The Evangelist" in *The Examiner*, 24 November 1887.

9. James D. Knowles, *Memoir of Mrs. Ann H. Judson* (Boston: Lincoln & Edmands, 1829), 18.

10. Henry H. Tucker, "A Pastor Seeking Light," in *Christian Index and Southwestern Baptist*, 12 February 1880, 2.

Chapter 6

1. Ernest F. Kevan, *The Grace of Law* (Ligonier, Pa.: Soli Deo Gloria Publications, 1993). Kevan's knowledge of the primary sources is comprehensive and the arrangement of topics in this book makes for the greatest facility of studying systematically the relationship of law and grace in the Puritan era. He includes several Baptist writers, e.g. Nehemiah Cox and John Bunyan, in his study.

2. "Circular Letter," The Elders and Messengers of the several Baptist Churches, etc. 1786, 1.

3. Andrew Fuller, *The Works of Andrew Fuller,* 3 vols. (Philadelphia: American Baptist Publication Society, n.d.), 2:661.

4. Keach, *The Everlasting Covenant,* 29.

5. John Ryland, Jr. *Serious Remarks on the Different Representations of Evangelical Doctrine by the Professing Friends of the Gospel,* Part the Second (Bristol: J. G. Fuller, 1818), 47–48.

6. Richard Furman, *Sermon on the Constitution and Order of the Christian Church* (Charleston: Markland & McIver, 1791), 26–27.

7. Charles D. Mallary, *Soul Prosperity: Its Nature, Its Fruits, and Its Culture,* reprint ed. (Harrisonburg, Va.: Sprinkle Publications, 1999; originally Charleston, S.C.: Southern Baptist Publication Society, 1860), 199–200.

8. Richard Fuller, "The Law and the Gospel," in *Sermons by Richard Fuller,* 3 vols. (Baltimore: John F. Weishampel, Jr.; Philadelphia: American Baptist Publication Society; New York: Sheldon and Company, 1877) 2:108–109.

9. Ibid., 1:246, 248.

10. Ibid., 2:333–334.

11. Frank Louis Mauldin *The Classic Baptist Heritage* (Franklin, Tenn.: Providence House Publishers, 1999), 30. Mauldin's citations and paraphrases of Hobson are from Hobson's work *A Discoverie of Truth* published in London in 1647 and *Practicall Divinitie* published in London in 1646. It is not the point of this discussion of Mauldin to correct what, in my opinion, are misapplications of Hobson but merely to show the tendency to antinomianism of the moderate view of freedom in Christ.

12. E. Glenn Hinson, *Are Southern Baptists "Evangelicals"?* (Macon: Mercer University Press, 1983), 173.

13. Harry Emerson Fosdick, *The Living of These Days* (New York: Harper & Brothers, 1956), 202.

14. Ibid., 203.

15. Ibid., 214–25.

Chapter 7

1. Avery Dulles, "Two Languages of Salvation: The Lutheran-Catholic Joint Declaration," *First Things* (December 1999), 26.

2. See *Canons and Decrees of the Council of Trent,* "Decree Concerning Justification," chapters 5–7, 14.

3. John Gano, "Circular Letter (on effectual calling)" in *Minutes of the Philadelphia Baptist Association, 1707 to 1807,* ed. A. D. Gillette (Springfield, Mo.: Particular Baptist Press, 2002), 201–202.

4. J. P. Boyce, *Abstract of Systematic Theology* (Philadelphia: American Baptist Publication Society, 1887), 367–68.

Chapter 8

1. A. D. Gillette, ed., *Minutes of the Philadelphia Baptist Association from 1707–1807* (Philadelphia: American Baptist Publication Society, 1851), 143.

2. This truth, central to the exposition of 2 Corinthians 3–4, as well as other passages, in theological nomenclature is known as *circumincessio* [L] or *perichoresis* [G].

3. Fuller, *Works*, 2:118.

4. Ibid., 2:119.

5. Ibid., 2:121.

6. Ibid.

7. Ibid., 2:175.

8. Ibid., 2:181–86.

9. Ibid., 2:191–92.

10. Charles Spurgeon, "Daniel's Band," in *Spurgeon's Expository Encyclopedia*, 15 vols. (Grand Rapids: Baker Book House, 1977), 6:38.

11. Charles H. Spurgeon, *Sword and Trowel*, 1865:3.

12. Charles H. Spurgeon, *New Park Street Pulpit*, 1859:141.

13. Charles H. Spurgeon, *New Park Street Pulpit*, 1855, 1.

14. "Articles of Religion" of the New Connection in William L. Lumpkin, *Baptist Confessions of Faith*, rev. ed. (Valley Forge: Judson Press, 1969), 343.

15. This discussion reflects the concerns of J. C. Means, "How a Declining Denomination May Be Saved from Extinction," in *The General Baptist Magazine*, December 1867, 353–58.

Chapter 9

1. R. Albert Mohler Jr., "Has Theology a Future in the SBC" in *Beyond the Impasse*, ed. Robison B. James and David S. Dockery (Nashville: Broadman Press, 1992), 99.

2. Timothy George, "Conflict and Identity in the SBC: A Quest for a New Consensus" in Robison and Dockery, 211.

3. John Spilsberie, *Gods Ordinance, The Saints Priviledge* (London, Printed by M. Simmons for Benjamin Allen, 1646) including *The Saints Interest by Christ in all the Privileges of Grace*, 26–27.

4. Oliver Hart, *A Gospel Church Portrayed and her Orderly Service Pointed Out* (Trenton: Printed by Isaac Collins, 1791), 19.

5. Benjamin Keach, *The Glory of a True Church and its Discipline Display'd* (London, 1697), 6.

6. *A Summary of Church Discipline* by the Baptist Association in Charleston, S.C., 12.

7. Richard Furman, *Constitution and Order of the Christian Church* (Charleston, S.C.: Markland & McIver, 1791), 8–10.

8. Ibid., 11.

9. J. P. Boyce, *Three Changes in Theological Institutions* (Greenville, S.C.: C. J. Elford's Book and Job Press, 1856), 34–35.

10. Ibid., 35.

11. Keach, *The Glory of a True Church*, 9.

12. William Rogers, *A Sermon Occasioned by the Death of the Rev. Oliver Hart* (Philadelphia: Printed by Lang and Ustick, 1796), 12–15.

13. Furman, *Constitution*, 23.

14. Ibid., 26–27.

15. W. B. Johnson, *The Gospel Developed Through the Government and Order of the Churches of Jesus Christ* (Richmond: K. Ellyson, 1846), 82.

16. Keach, *Glory*, 32.

17. Ibid., 34.

18. *The Minutes of the Philadelphia Baptist Association*, 58.

19. *A Summary of Church Discipline*, 26.

20. Furman, *Constitution*, 12–13.

21. P. H. Mell. *Corrective Church Discipline* (Athens: The E. D. Stone Press, 1912 [reprint from the 1860 edition]), 12.

22. B. R. White, ed., *Association Records of the Particular Baptists of England, Wales and Ireland to 1660*, 3 Parts (London: Baptist Historical Society, 1971), 3:95.

Chapter 10

1. E. Y. Mullins, *Why is Christianity True?* (Philadelphia: American Baptist Publication Society, 1905), 57.

2. Ibid., 32.

3. L. Russ Bush, *The Advancement: Keeping the Faith in an Evolutionary Age* (Nashville: Broadman & Holman, 2003), 85.

4. B. R. White, ed., *Associated Records of the Particular Baptists of England, Wales, and Ireland to 1600*, 3 parts (London: Baptist Historical Society, 1971), 1:35.

5. Ibid., 3:94.

6. Ibid., 3:98.

7. Mallary, *Soul Prosperity: Its Fruits, and Its Culture*, reprint ed. (Harrisonville, Va.: Sprinkle Publications, 1999; originally Charleston, S.C.: Southern Baptist Publication Society, 1860), 295, 297, 299.

8. Ibid., 25–26.

Epilogue

1. Mallary, *Soul Prosperity*, 297.

2. I use this word with a special nuance. It does not indicate an "I don't care" flippancy about the good of the church. It indicates that factors of organizational efficiency began to crowd out the theological concerns of building a church. Gaines Dobbins, (*The Efficient Church: A Study of Polity and Methods in the Light of New Testament Principles and Modern Conditions and Needs.* Nashville: Sunday School Board of the Southern Baptist Convention, 1923), gave detailed attention to the New Testament authority on every issue of church ministry. At times, however, his drive for efficiency led him to endorse some theologically questionable activities in pursuit of a more active church. (e.g., "The Enlistment Ideal," 183–86). The desire for efficiency and immediacy increasingly dominated Southern Baptist thinking from that time throughout the twentieth century. Organization and marketable methods rendered theological reflection and application less and less important.

3. Martin Luther, *The Complete Sermons of Martin Luther*, 7 vols., ed. John Nicholas Lenker, trans., John Nicholas Lenker and others (Grand Rapids: Baker Book House, 2000), 3:39–40.